When God Called
Piper *home*

Also by Julie Brawner:

The Coach's Wife Study Guide

—A companion study guide for *The Coach's Wife*
by Carolyn Allen

When God Called Piper home

a true story of love, loss, and God's sweet comfort

JULIE BRAWNER

WestBow
PRESS
A DIVISION OF THOMAS NELSON

ISBN: 978-1-4497-4765-7 (e)
ISBN: 978-1-4497-4766-4 (sc)
ISBN: 978-1-4497-4767-1 (hc)

Library of Congress Control Number: 2012906486

WestBow Press books may be ordered through booksellers or by contacting:

WestBow Press
A Division of Thomas Nelson
1663 Liberty Drive
Bloomington, IN 47403
www.westbowpress.com
1-(866) 928-1240

Thank you to my sweet Susan G. Mathis, editor. Thank you for choosing to undertake this project with me, for editing the manuscript, and turning simple pages written in a word document into the book before us. You have blessed us beyond words. You have gently taken the story of pain and helped turn it into a masterpiece to share with the world.

Printed in the United States of America

WestBow Press rev. date: 4/26/2012

Dave and I dedicate this book to our sweet Piper Kay
and to her friends Kyle Joseph, Caroline Joy, and Holden
Newell who are rejoicing with her in the heavens.

We also dedicate this to all the parents who have endured the
pain of seeing their child go to heaven before them.

We all long to see you again, little ones.

Contents

Forward

By Lindsay Turner

When I first saw Julie Brawner at the beginning of the year teachers' meeting in the library of the elementary school where she was a new hire and I a returning teacher, I hardly noticed the spunky little bright-eyed woman with her short wispy hair and glasses. In fact, I'm not even really sure that I managed to mutter a decent "good morning" to her on that first morning back to work after a long summer break. Yet we soon became fast and dear friends.

That first day, I certainly had no idea that in just a few years we would be more than just friends and co-workers, that we would form a bond that made us more like sisters, and that I would be one of the first people to hold her precious first daughter, Adia. And I never would have imagined that just a few years down the road, I would also hear her sobbing on the other end of the phone as she told me the terrible news that she and her husband, Dave, had lost their second daughter at the very end of her pregnancy, and that in the days to come we would lean on each other, cry together, and become even more like a family.

The summer before her tragic loss, Julie and I had spent our summer vacation taking Adia to the aquarium, enjoying cupcakes at the park, and planning a nursery for the new baby, Piper. We had held a shower for the beautiful baby girl that we were so anxious to spoil along with her sister. Now, every time I think of that sweet baby shower, tears come to my eyes.

The Brawners were such a young, happy family rejoicing in their baby's imminent arrival. There was not a cloud on the horizon. So the inability to find the baby's heartbeat that day hit everyone with the force of a runaway train.

The death of a healthy, full-term infant often provokes a string of unanswerable questions and terrifying thoughts. What-if's creep into a previously stable mind set. "What if the doctor had just taken her early?" "What if I had eaten better, exercised more or less?" "What if I had remembered to take all of the pre-natal vitamins?"

The death of Piper also provoked a barrage of questions in my own mind. Why would a family so deserving have something so precious torn away from them? My anger was only fueled by the recent birth of a beautiful, healthy baby— to a girl that I had known all through school and who had just been released from prison after years of drug addiction! She got pregnant by accident. She had a healthy baby. She gave that baby away without a backwards glance—just days after we lost Piper.

Julie and Dave Brawner are two of the best, most godly people I've ever met. Their outlook is always positive: their compassion is always evident. I honestly think that if there is anybody in the world who deserves a life filled with blessings, it is the two of them.

So when they faced such a tragedy, I was angry. I was confused. I was heartbroken. But through the sadness and the challenges we faced together, Julie and Dave continued to teach me with their example.

Yes, they were hurt. They were confused. They were heartbroken. But somehow, they never, ever lost hope. They never questioned God's love for them. They did not let bitterness take hold of them and drag them down.

As a mother, I cannot even begin to imagine the pain of losing a child. But I know that if I were faced with such pain, I would want Julie there next to me, holding my hand and reminding me that it is okay to hurt. She would assure me that I would make it and that there is hope. I think that writing this book was Julie's way of "holding hands" with hurting women everywhere.

May her book offer perspective, hope, and honesty in the midst of a tragedy that may seem hopeless. With God, it is not.

Acknowledgements

Thank you to Christa Wells and Natalie Grant for writing and recording a song that ministered so deeply to my soul. I hope that by sharing your lyrics through this book, more lives will be touched for the glory of God.

Thank you to Now I Lay Me Down to Sleep Ministries and to Carol Howard for being a solid rock on the day Piper was born, for taking pictures that will forevermore bless the hearts of those who can see our precious baby girl, and for allowing me to use them in this book—front cover and all!

Thank you to Chet and Sarah Erwin for sharing true life through the ministry of Holden Uganda, and for allowing us to be a part of building a well in Piper's honor through the Barner's financial gifts.

To our friends and family, thank you for encouraging me to take this step to reach the hearts of many with the hope of Christ Jesus. Thank you for making this book possible, through your hopes, prayers, and support. Thank you to my mom and dad for financially making this dream a reality. Thank you to all for sticking with us and never letting go. Thank you for being our Team Piper.

Most of all, thank you to my husband, Dave, and to my firstborn, Adia. To my precious husband, you have been the only man I ever wish to walk beside. You have been my best friend, and one day, I will smile as I watch you twirl our Piper Kay around, after showing her how to dribble the basketball up the court and perfect her three-pointer. You bless me every moment of every day.

And to our sweet Adia Michele—you are truly God's gift to your dad and me. You are like Jesus in so many ways. Your smile lights up the room, and your personality blesses us daily. We love you, and we are proud of you. We know that God has magnificent things in store for you throughout your life, just as God has for Piper in her death. You would have been an amazing older sister to Piper. Know that she loves you, and never forget how much we cherish you.

Thank you that when we confess with our mouths that Jesus is Lord and believe in our hearts that you raised him from the dead, we can hold to your truth in Romans ten—and know that we will be saved. Please, Father, use this for your glory.

In Christ's love and by his grace alone,

Julie

whengodcalledpiperhome@gmail.com

Preface

We had no idea that our lives would be so drastically changed on the hot summer day in July. Forevermore, the moments of everyday life now seem so radically different. Through the twists and turns of pain, the agony of mourning, and facing the depths of my soul that I did not know existed, I can kneel before God and say, "I believe!"

The song, "Held," written by Christa Wells and recorded by Natalie Grant, resonated so deeply in my soul that I felt compelled to write. As I began journaling, the tug of our Savior seemed to say, "Child, it's time to write."

From the resounding echoes of a hurting heart came the chapters that lay before you. They are chapters of truth, hurt, loss, pain, suffering, and hope. I refused to cover up the depth of agony that digs through the soul of one who has lost a child. Yet as I wrote these pages, in complete and utter honesty, I soon began to share my heart with others. And they began to share with others. And now, I wish to share with you.

Come and sit with me a while at the feet of our Christ Jesus.

Chapter One

Held

"The Lord is a shelter for the oppressed, a refuge in times of trouble. Those who know your name trust in you, for you, O LORD, do not abandon those who search for you," Psalm 9:9-10 (NLT).

The words from the song, "Held," written by Christa Wells and recorded by Natalie Grant resound in my heart like a constant echo. "This is what it means to be held, how it feels, when the sacred is torn from your life and you survive." The rest of the song fades away, but those words remain.

As I sit holding my oldest daughter, Adia, I am reminded of my younger one, Piper, who I buried just a few short weeks ago. As I lay Adia down in her bed, my heartfelt prayer engulfs the room. *Lord, hold Adia in your arms tonight. Rock her to sleep, and let her know your touch—just as Piper knows it.*

I feel like I should be sitting in a therapy circle, introducing myself. "Hello. My name is Julie Brawner, and I have lost a child."

Although I have experienced what I would never, ever wish upon another, I am still blessed to have a sweet princess, Adia, sleeping soundly in the room next to me. I am a mother. I have birthed two sweet babies. We are now in "the terrible twos" with

Adia Michele, and through deep sorrow, we realize that we will never get to experience any of these stages with our Piper Kay.

We are walking the road of parenting—through life and through death. My dream? My hope? To share with every woman, mother, and parent of any child —that life is but many little, precious, and fleeting moments. Seize every one as if it were your last. It just might be.

Our story is unusual.

You may be reading this and have numerous friends or family members pop into your head. "I know a girl that…" or "My sister went through …"

What I have learned is that, although there are many similar situations when it comes to losing someone you love, every single loss is different. Each has earned its sacred place of validity. You cannot compare one loss of a child to another.

Every story is unique.

Each and every loss is a book in itself. The pain is very much similar, but the stories—the words written in God's Book of Life—are unique to every child, every family, and every mother. In some moments, our stories may seem comparable. In others, they are drastically different.

It seems that, only moments ago, we received the news that we had lost Piper Kay. And yet at times it seems that every second of every day drags on as if it has already been a lifetime.

The Perfect Pregnancy until…

Our precious two-year-old daughter, Adia, shares a birthday with her daddy in July. When we found out that, although unplanned, we were expecting our second baby girl—and she would share the same birthday month as her daddy and sister—we were so excited.

It was a perfect pregnancy, along with the perfect fifty pounds of weight gain and the lovely swollen feet and ankles I experienced.

Everything was normal. Every test came back flawless. Piper was right on target, due July 30, 2011.

Since the pregnancy was unplanned, we were a bit panicked about adding this fourth member to our family. Yet over the nine months of Piper kicking and spinning and doing her dance moves inside me, we fell in love with her.

We wondered what it would be like to have two little darlings spinning around our living room. The baby's room was set up; her sign with her name was hung over her crib; and her Winnie the Pooh mobile was hanging—although it was missing a few choice characters, thanks to her sister.

I spent the summer taking Adia to the aquarium or to the children's museum. It was such a hot summer that there was not much fun to be had outside. July 26 finally rolled around. This day was like all the rest; it was smoldering hot outside.

I had taken Adia to her school for the day, and my friend Mindy had come into town to hang out with me. Little did she know what she'd experience with me that day. Nor did I know what a divine plan it was for her to be with me.

Dave was out of town on an interview that morning, and I had planned on heading to my regular weekly doctor's appointment after we had done our laundry at the laundromat. Since we had moved from our apartment to a townhome that weekend, we had yet to find a washer and dryer. We had spent the entire weekend setting up the girls' rooms and making sure the house was ready for the lively two year old and her infant sister, so we had plenty of sweaty clothes to wash.

As we waited for the wash to finish, I rubbed my belly and recalled the green and pink room waiting for Piper. Then I realized that Mindy and I wouldn't have enough time to dry the clothes before the appointment. So we packed up the wet clothes and headed to the appointment, with the plan of hitting the dryers after my routine check-up was over.

Shockingly, my life was about to change—forever.

As Mindy and I sat in my doctor's office, the doctor asked how things were. I wanted to ask, "Can we just induce? Get this girl out! We're ready, and it's hot!" Instead, I told her that I hadn't really been feeling the baby move very much lately. But that was normal during the end of the pregnancy, right? She was growing and running out of room!

The doctor looked at me and asked me if I had tried the "juice trick"—to give the baby a little sugar high and encourage her to move. I told her that I had slurped down a juice box, laid on my left side, and waited to see if Piper would start attempting somersaults. She didn't. But I told the doctor, "She's out of room in there!"

The doctor looked at me with a little concern. Then the nurse moved me to a different room, laid me down, and began to search for the baby's heartbeat. The nurse shook the machine and said, "This machine is old. Let me get the newer one. I'm so bad at this!"

I thought nothing of it, but then the doctor came in and did the same with the "newer" device, to no avail. When the doctor switched on the ultrasound machine I started thinking, *Maybe I need an emergency C-section. Maybe Piper is coming today!*

The doctor did not flinch, one way or another, and she sent me to the hospital just down the road to get another, more intensive ultrasound done. The doctor simply said, "I couldn't see everything I wanted to see here on my machine. So just walk up to the hospital desk, and they'll get you in right away."

As Mindy and I climbed into the car and drove to the hospital, I looked at Mindy and asked, "There's no way–I haven't lost Piper, right? That just doesn't happen now, does it? She's nine months along. Less than a week ago, she checked out fine! Nothing could have happened in that short amount of time, could it?"

We nodded to each other, confident that Piper was ready to meet the world!

I walked briskly into the medical center, only to be told

that I needed to sign in and take a seat. "We will call you," the receptionist said all too casually. I tapped my foot feverishly until my name was finally called—not for the ultrasound—but for my insurance! *What? Did I not "pre-register" here for a reason?* I thought. *I am positive that I did all this paperwork already!*

I looked across the desk at the orders for my ultrasound and saw "STAT" in bold red letters across the top of the chart.

Do they not see that? Do they not know that I may need an emergency C-section? I thought. *They should be putting me on a stretcher and wheeling me back to cut me open and get Piper out!*

All I heard was "Wa wa wa wa wa wa" and "Please sign here" as my heart groaned and panicked and prayed.

Finally, after what seemed to be an eternity, Mindy and I walked in for the ultrasound. But as we began to enter the room, the technician refused to let Mindy come in with me! "Family only! Is she family?" I growled under my breath and walked into the room—alone. Behind closed doors, the technician slowly and all too casually found the paperwork, put on her glasses, and asked, "So, why are you here today?"

What? Are you seriously going to sit there and ask me that right now? I thought I was about to scream! Controlling my emotions to the best of my ability, I attempted to calmly tell her that the doctor seemed a bit worried, and that she was not sure about a heartbeat... and that the paperwork for an ultrasound said "STAT"! I pointed to the large red letters on her paper.

She looked at me and asked, "So when was your last menstrual period?"

I looked at her in horror and said with exasperation and sass, "I have no idea." Eventually, we got around to the "STAT" ultrasound. She never let me see the screen. She did not say a word. She typed away on her little keypad as I attempted to text my husband. But there was no cell service the little room.

It was just the quiet ultrasound tech, God, and me. I was numb, confused, and very alone. *Lord, what is going on? I need them to cut me open and get Piper out! There is obviously something wrong. Can you please hurry them up?*

The tech said that she'd call the doctor, and she asked me to head back to the doctor's office. As Mindy and I headed back to the doctor's office to hear the results, I still thought, *This just doesn't happen. Nine months. She's fully cooked. She's here. She's ready. And six days ago I was in this same office, listening to her heartbeat and watching the doctor say, "Sounds great!"*

Yet God knew—and he had covered me already—with his peace that I would come to know so deeply in the days ahead.

I sat there in the doctor's office as she told me, in tears, that Piper Kay had gone to be with our Lord Jesus Christ. With hot tears of confusion and disbelief rolling down my face, she told me it was nothing I did or didn't do. I calmly nodded at her words. My chest heaved in and out as I told myself to keep breathing. I tried to listen as she told me that this tragedy was a mystery. I cried when she leaned over, held my hand, and prayed with me. Complete and utter shock hit my wounded heart.

It was God's ultimate plan...yet we will never understand why.

And at that moment I knew, "This is what it means to be held."

Chapter Two

Our Journey Begins

"This is what it means to be held, how it feels,
when the sacred is torn from your life and you
survive. This is what it is to be loved and to know
that the promise was that when everything fell,
we'd be held. If hope is born of suffering; if this
is only the beginning; can we not wait, for one
hour, watching for our Savior? This is what it
means to be held..."

> —From the song "Held" recorded by Natalie
> Grant and written by Christa Wells.

I feel compelled to sit and write. I have an overwhelming urge
to run to the mountaintops and shout from the depths of my
soul, "Hear me out!" We've lost a child. In utter shock.

If you're reading this, you may have faced a similar loss, and
you know how it hurts.

There was no time to decide if we would carry her to full
term. We were given no warning or lead time to consciously
make extra effort to coddle her in the womb. Within moments,
our lives were changed—forever. And in the midst of such heart-
wrenching pain, I want to sit with you a while. I want to drink
a cup of coffee with you, cry together, and tell you...God is
enough.

As the Lord's strength picked me up, helped me out of the doctor's office, and carried me to my car that day, He whispered in my ear, "I've got you Julie." I called my husband in shock, practically out of breath, and I told him, "We've lost Piper."

I have never heard a man sob and weep like I heard my husband do that day. He was twenty minutes from me, on his way back from the interview. And he wept.

Our souls were overwhelmed. And yet His blanket of peace covered us.

The drive home was filled with disbelief, but Mindy's silent presence was a comfort nonetheless. After she dropped me home, she sweetly took my wet laundry, dried it, and brought it back to me before she headed home.

My emotions were rolling. What just happened? What do I do now?

Then a feeling of embarrassment hit me. I've got this huge belly. I should be giving birth and bringing home a baby girl. And now...I'm not. People will look at me and expect a little car seat to be placed in the back of my Jeep, and there will never be one.

I brushed it off—as an emotion I would have to deal with later, and I attempted to think. *How do I make these phone calls? Everyone is wondering how my appointment went. They're waiting eagerly to hear that Piper is on her way! And now this.* Again, embarrassment flooded in. Yet I picked up my phone and dialed those near and dear to my heart...and in tears, friends and family began to rally around us.

Within hours, our house was filled with people who were rubbing my belly, crying, hugging, and mourning. I remember putting Adia to bed that night, and later crawling in mine and pulling a blanket over my head—weeping like I never knew I could. I remember hands surrounding me, holding me...holding us.

Why did I have to carry her one more night? Why didn't

they check me into the hospital right away and take her then? Because.

God knew. We needed that one more night with Piper Kay.

We needed to spend those hours massaging her little body, kissing her through the womb, spilling our tears, and telling her we loved her. I know she was gone, but we needed that—for us.

And as 4 a.m. rolled around, we got up in the darkness of that early July morning to "walk the plank"...or so it felt.

The drive to the hospital was gut wrenching. I clung to my husband's hand and he to mine. Our eyes were swollen from the amount of tears we had shed together. Our eyelids looked as if we'd had some Botox done the night before. We pulled up, seemingly the only people at the hospital at that early hour.

It is awful—going into the hospital and everyone knowing the outcome of the birth to come. My paperwork would pass through hands, and they would look at Dave and me with sadness.

As we continued to cling to one another, the nurses began to induce labor. I lay there in a dark room, surrounded by people I loved, and yet I felt so alone. Tears fell down my face and soaked the lovely maternity gown I was wearing. I lay there knowing that contractions would soon start and that in the end, we'd go home—just the two of us.

But praise God for a labor and delivery that went so quickly and perfectly, at least in comparison to my previous delivery. There were no complications apart from not getting an epidural due to Piper coming so quickly!

I remember pushing that last time and seeing Piper's lifeless body fall onto the table—an image I will never forget. There was my baby girl, lying in the doctor's hands. There was no breath, no life, and no sweet cry.

She lay there limp and colorless, and yet as I gazed upon her form, I was amazed. Our Piper Kay.

She was beautiful—as beautiful as any baby has been. Her face was perfect, with a nose just like her daddy's. She had all

9

her fingers and toes. She was 6 lbs. 12 oz. and 21 inches, long and lean. She would have been her daddy's post player on his basketball team. She had a full head of hair, a beautiful mouth like her sister's. She was perfect.

I remember thinking, *Surely if we just hold her long enough, she will begin to breathe! Surely...surely.*

There was no cord wrapped around any part of her body. There was nothing wrong with the placenta. There were no answers, and there never will be. It was her time.

Piper's days had been written in the Book of Life, and they were numbered. God called our Piper Kay to come home to him, for he knew that through her death, lives would be eternally altered. And as we held her in that room, a room filled with more peace than I could have ever imagined, we sang to her, loved her, and made memories that will last for the journey ahead—a life without our Piper.

I remember the night before, being asked, "Are you going to hold her? Are you going to take pictures? Is Adia going to come and see her?" Dave and I looked at each other in horror. "No! No! It's too painful..."

But God quickly melted our hearts and changed our horror into blessings.

We *did* hold Piper Kay. We *did* take pictures. We *did* bring Adia up to the hospital to see her sister, and she sat with us holding Piper. Adia found her sister's eyes, her nose, and her mouth. She hugged her baby sister and smiled at her. She oohed and awed over the "baby" that lay in her lap. And when they took Piper's lifeless body out of the grip of her sister, Adia screamed, and tears ran down her face. She didn't want to let her go of baby Piper. And neither did we.

We have always sung to our sweet Adia before bed, "Now we lay Adia down to sleep. We pray thee Lord, my child to keep. Thy love guard her through the night, and wake her with the morning light." I'm sure the words are completely wrong. And

I'm positive that the tune her father and I sing is most incorrect. But, it's the Brawner-version of our special song.

So as Dave held Piper Kay Brawner, all 6 lbs. 12 oz. of her, there came the moment when we had to say goodbye. And as we touched the head of our baby girl, we could not say goodbye. Instead, we sang to her…and we sang.

"Now we lay Piper down to sleep. We pray thee Lord, our child to keep. Thy love guard her through the night, and wake her with the morning light." Through broken, choppy words, we choked out the song to our daughter.

Bawling, Dave took his baby girl and handed her to the nurse. As her lifeless body was wheeled away, our hearts were shredded, wounded beyond any feeling imaginable. We knew that we would never again see or hold our Piper Kay on this earth. We knew that we must wait our lifetime till we reach heaven.

Our road has been marked with suffering. And yet in the midst of this suffering, I know God has a plan.

As I share our journey, and as you walk this road with us, life alters just a bit. Things become clearer. As you will later stand at the top of the mountain with me and take in the view, I hope you will begin to realize that so many things that might seem to matter now are insignificant when viewed in the reality of eternity.

I want you to journey to that mountaintop with me.

We may stumble along the way, bruise our knees, or roll our ankles. We may sit and cry together in complete raw emotion. We may even backslide at times. But what I know is this—we will not be alone.

As we walk this journey of life, not only can we choose to walk together, but we can be sure that our God walks right next to us. He steadies our feet, he bandages our wounds, he tapes our ankles, and he says, "Come child. I will help you. I will sit with you. I will listen."

So with that image imprinted in your mind, of us sitting at

the edge of the mountain and looking up at the journey ahead, my prayer—my hearts cry—is that you would come to know that His words are truth. They really are. And although we may claim to believe, I hope that raw emotions will stir your soul and that God will touch you to the depths, leaving your faith stronger and your heart longing for heaven.

As Natalie Grant's chorus rings in my heart, I am certain that "This is what it is to be loved and to know that the promise was that when everything fell…we'd be held." I pray you will know that, too.

Chapter Three

Entrusted With Life and Death

"So commit yourselves wholeheartedly to these words of mine. Tie them to your hands and wear them on your forehead as reminders. Teach them to your children. Talk about them when you are at home and when you are on the road, when you are going to bed and when you are getting up. Write them on the doorposts of your house and on your gates, so that as long as the sky remains above the earth, you and your children may flourish in the land the LORD swore to give your ancestors," Deuteronomy 11:18-21 (NLT).

I am blessed to come home to a daughter that is…well, a pistol. Our Adia is a fireball. She always has been and hopefully, always will be. She is opinionated, feisty, and frankly a little OCD. She runs around with little figurines—like her Winnie the Pooh and Tigger or her Woody and Jesse—and makes them slide, fall, jump, or run. Whatever her imagination has for them that day is what they will be doing.

Dave and I were more than ecstatic about having another little girl to join her playtime. After we lost Piper, we came home and realized that life will never be the same—ever.

Piper's room will never be filled with giggles and coos. The recliner will never rock her little body. Her swing will never hold her. And yet, in the room next door, we look in the face of our breathing, living daughter, and we realize we cannot sit here in grief and agony all day long. We must get up, pick up our mat, and walk.

Most women will someday be mothers. Whether they birth the child or adopt, women typically have a desire to love and raise a child of their own. When we found out about losing Piper, my husband's first instinct was to pick up Adia and bring her home, although soaked in a bath of his own tears, and protect her. He is a father. I am a mother. And we are parents of two.

Although we have lost our baby girl, she was ours. She will always be ours. We are a family of four—we just had to bury one.

I am just like any other woman in this world who has birthed two children. I am a mother of two, and always will be. Just because Piper Kay Brawner never breathed the air of this world does not negate the fact that she is my daughter. Just because we didn't get to laugh and play with her, dance with her, or walk her down the aisle doesn't mean she is not our very own. And just because Adia didn't get to teach her about Winnie the Pooh, sing to her, or run in the sprinklers and twirl her, doesn't mean she is not her sister. Although we have lost her, she is still ours.

As we walk through this valley, there have been many loved ones who have chosen to stumble along this path with us. They've put on their hiking shoes, grabbed their walking stick, and said, "Let's go." And we are grateful.

At times, these dear people have had to lift me up and carry me, just like what Aaron did for Moses in Exodus seventeen. When Moses could no longer hold his own arms up, Aaron came alongside him and provided help in time of need. And these sweet friends who have walked beside me? Most are mothers. Many have baby girls at home, lying in their beds, breathing in and out every night. Am I jealous? Should they feel bad that they have their child, living and breathing, and I've buried mine?

Oh, sweet, sweet friends...No!

I am overwhelmed with a sense of urgency to share what I have learned. I desire to run alongside each of you, holding your babies, loving your children, and living life with you.

Life can change in an instant. In the blink of an eye, the path that you've so neatly planned for your life can be altered. Nothing is a guarantee.

So take time NOW. Take time—in every moment—to love your child. You have been given a gift—the breath and life of your child. Honor God with it! And as he or she grows, remember... your child is entrusted to you and is in your care to raise in the goodness of our God. And THAT is the most important thing in life. That is what we need to sacrifice for.

May our children know the goodness of our God, and may they spend eternity in his arms, just as Piper now is!

Why do we run so fast in this life and not take time to smell the daisies? Adia is very good at stopping to "smell." Yet too often I have discouraged her from doing so. I've gotten frustrated. "Come on, Adia. We've got to go!" Really? We do?

We rush ourselves through life, and our children see that. We go so fast, so furiously, that the real meanings of life tend to get pushed to the wayside, and we leave no time for the important things. With our iPhones out, we may find ourselves spending more time on those and less time investing in the lives of our living and breathing...who sit wide eyed just waiting for time with their mommy and daddy.

God did not create life to be rushed through. He did not desire stress, anxiety, and frustrations to overwhelm our daily routine. As believers, if we truly say we know him, should we not take a step back, look at our lives, and ask ourselves, "Are we honoring him in all we do?"

At church recently, Dave and I cried through the service, but I left with this message:

For every 'yes,' we say 'no' to something.

And this has stuck with me. For every time we say 'yes' to something, even though it may very well be good, we are saying 'no' to something else. Dave and I sat down and talked about how we needed to apply this to our lives.

Every time he says 'yes' to staying late at school for open gym, he's saying 'no' to coming home to our family. Every time I say 'yes' to staying late at school to grade papers (that I should have done during my conference time), I'm saying 'no' to picking up Adia a few minutes earlier.

And because of our recent experience, I am painfully aware that minutes do mean everything.

When we say 'yes' to staying home and spending time with our family over the weekend, we're saying 'no' to traveling in the car and seeing friends. And that's okay.

For every 'yes' we say 'no' to something—it's a hard but true statement. I know that sometimes it's unavoidable; sometimes we have to stay late at work. But as we sat and talked about this, Dave decided to open the gym twice a week for a little longer rather than three times a week for a shorter amount of time. Why? Because that meant only two nights he would be at the gym—not three—and we'd have more precious time together.

Still, we miss having time with our Piper Kay, and although we will always experience that emptiness, we know she is in the best place. She is in heaven, with her Heavenly Father. We know that she is being given everything we could imagine for her and so much more. She has no fear, no pain, and no tears.

Our little Piper never knew sin. She never endured a skinned knee, or a slammed finger. She has breathed only the purity of our Savior and known the rejoicing songs of our God.

Piper Kay's name means "Joyous spirit; rejoicing," and we know full well that she is already living up to her name.

Adia Michele means "God's gift; like God," and she too will live up to her name here on earth.

We are parents of two. I am a mother of two. I love my baby girls. I always will. And I have realized that mothering is a gift to be treasured.

I know. You've heard it before. But really, I mean it! I've looked in the face of death, and now I understand…this life is so fragile! My breathing baby girl? I've been entrusted to handle her with care. And my second baby girl? I've been entrusted to trust God with her.

So as I look down from this mountain and take in life's view, I want you to look too. Breath is not promised. Life is so short. Grab your child, whether young or old, and draw them to you. Tell them you love them, hold them close, and teach them the ways of eternity.

Take time to smell the daisies, and teach them to do the same. This life is a mere spec in the view of eternity. Journey with them, while you still have breath.

Chapter Four

Will You Stay?

"Then a despised Samaritan came along, and when he saw the man, he felt compassion for him. Going over to him, the Samaritan soothed his wounds with olive oil and wine and bandaged them. Then he put the man on his own donkey and took him to an inn, where he took care of him," Luke 10:33-34 (NLT).

I never thought driving by a cemetery would make me tear up as quickly as it does now. A quick glance at the headstones and flowers brings a flood of memories.

Making funeral arrangements for a baby is...sad.

The casket we chose for Piper was a precious little white one. When we saw it at the funeral home, my heart sunk. It was so tiny. Pink Gerber daisies were laid preciously along the top.

I remember the drive to the cemetery the morning we buried her. It was a long drive, and as we pulled up, there were cars on every side in every direction. We were honored and humbled as we attempted to squeeze through the mass amount of cars to find a parking spot. What a blessing!

People drove from all over to hear the truth of Piper Kay— to know that she had gone to be with our Savior, and he was holding her. They celebrated her and showed up wearing pink and white.

It was comforting to know that people were willing to drive, to be there, to experience pain alongside us. We needed every one of them who were willing to stand with us...as we realized once again—the shock. This is for real.

We released butterflies that day in memory of our Piper Kay.

Natalie Grant's recorded song "Held," played as Adia helped hold the box of butterflies. The joy on her face was priceless as she released them. The hill country was filled with the words of the song as it played loudly. The butterflies took flight and rose to the heavens. Piper's tiny, white casket was front and center. Just a peek at it from afar, and hearts were broken.

Butch Smith, our friend and pastor from college, spoke, both blessing and challenging the crowd. He spoke truths from the book of Job. He spoke of truth from the word of God. He encouraged others to have faith, and he begged all to choose Christ that day. This man, who is like family to us, shared this poem he had written, and then he prayed:

Piper Kay Brawner

Life too short! Too short! Too very short!

Hearts broken! Tears shed!

We call her Piper! We love! We lost! We grieve! We believe!

From the womb you knew! You formed!

You let end! She is gone! She is with you, her spirit in heaven!

~ ~ ~

We do not understand your ways, but we trust you, God! So grant us wisdom and perspective, we pray.

We ask for help and healing, for our hearts hurt. Your grace is our need in this time of heartbreak. Please come, and grant us your peace in turmoil!

Awaken our hearts and minds to your ways. Let us see your working in all this pain. We need your presence today, right now. Come meet with us, and grant us wisdom to live, to love, to laugh, and to grieve for your glory.

We need you Savior, Lord Jesus, because your yoke is easy, and your burden is light. So we rest in you by grace and through faith that you are loving and in complete control.

We cry out to you, asking for help, healing, clarity, and hope in despair. Come Lord Jesus, and heal our hearts so that we may grieve fully and well, for we see that this life is just too short.

—By Butch Smith

Pastor Ray Still, from Oakwood Baptist Church in New Braunfels, shared about how Jesus loves the little children and how he was certain that Jesus is holding Piper right now. He shared about how Christ would call the children to him, and he would take time to sit with them.

You could sense the encouragement that those words gave. Those surrounding us began to envision Piper in his arms, the warmest, most hopeful place she could be. Dave's sister, Mollie, shared the most beautiful part of her heart to the crowd. There was not a dry eye in those Hill County Gardens that day. There was not a heart untouched by God's hand.

Piper's little body was buried in "God's Little Garden", a part of Hill Country Memorial Gardens Cemetery that is designated for precious infants. She was laid to rest by the white picket fence that surrounds many little ones that have gone to heaven before her. It was all too real. As we spent time that week making sure her gravesite was beautiful, the ground became showered in our tears.

What just happened?

Only days ago we had been setting up her room, ready for her to come home. Now, we were kneeling before a headstone that says, "Piper Kay Brawner—July 27, 2011."

My heart now breaks for others who experience any kind of pain—like it has never broken before. Because of the depth of hurt and loss that we have experienced, even the slightest injury inflicted upon another is so painful to me.

When I see a friend hurting or panicked, my heart hurts with theirs. When I notice someone crying in church, my chest tightens, and I begin to pray for him or her. When others around me seemed stressed, I yearn to calm them.

Why am I so tenderhearted? What is this inside of me? I've been touched by the hand of God in a way that I've never known before. It feels like my heart has been consumed by his love and it no longer beats on its own. Every day my Jesus wakes me up, moves my feet—one behind the other—and pumps my heart.

He says, "Go, sweet girl. Walk." And I do. I am conscious of every breath. I feel the impact of every step taken.

You know that life has drastically changed when the Disney movie, "Tangled," makes you cry. There is a part in the movie when the parents release lanterns in hopes of finding their long lost daughter, and she finally finds home. Tears rolled down my face. My husband and I had to grab Kleenexes when we watched it with our two year old. We fast-forwarded through the semi-creepy parts (from a two-year-old's vantage point) and ended with tears filling our eyes as the family embraced, reunited as one again. We realized what a beautiful portrayal of the embrace we will experience one day with our Piper.

But until then, every July 27, Piper will see butterflies released—as a reminder of the hope we have of seeing her again.

A cemetery. A headstone. A heartbreak.

When I look through my tear-filled eyes, I realize that Piper's is not the only body that has been buried. There is so much sadness and death in this world. I know I'm not alone. If I could carry this burden for everyone, if I could take this yoke upon me so that no other would have to endure the loss of his or her child—I would.

Although every story is different, every loss is the same. We hurt. And we survive—but not without tremendous loss.

If you have ever experienced loss, you know there are days when life seems to remain a haze. You understand the zombie-like moments where all you can do is exist. Feelings of pure sorrow overwhelm, and there seem to be no more tears to pour out.

Most of us, in such a time of loss, crave the extended hand of someone nearby, someone to care. A squeeze on the shoulder or a hug...even tears would be appreciated. But what tends to happen is that in the midst of tragedy, people begin to flee. They just don't know what to do. And although some family members stay close, many who have faced this hardship with you will run. Why? Because we who have lost are plagued by a mark of death, so people tend to avoid us. We are wounded, and it's just hard for them to know how to help.

We simply require effort to make it through our days, and we need tremendous amounts of practical and emotional help along the way. We are no longer an "easy" load to carry. We are full of drama, and people can't handle it.

I often feel like I'm the wounded one in the story of the

Good Samaritan, and people are walking by me. They step over or around me; they make sure that they don't come too close; and they may even find a path that re-routes them completely.

As one who is hurt, wounded, and has lost something precious, I am lying on the path—broken, battered, and bruised. I do not possess the strength to even open my eyes sometimes. My body is water-deprived; my lungs are filled with dust; and my eyes are crusted shut from the heat of the sun beating down on me. Yet as I lay there so alone, crying out but with no tears left, I hear a voice:

"I'm here. And I'm going to stay."

I feel my body being lifted, placed on a donkey, and as I zone in and out of consciousness, I realize I am moving. I am going somewhere...and I am with someone. Water is lifted to my mouth and I am forced to drink small sips. Finally, in a bed with soft sheets, I realize that someone has taken the time to use a warm cloth and wipe away the crust from my eyes. As I open my eyes for the first time in days, I see that there are bandages wrapped around my cuts, and instead of being clothed in tattered cloth, there is a beautiful robe to cover me.

Hearing that same voice, I look up. Who is this who has chosen to clothe me? Who is this who has tenderly cared so much? Who is this who instead of walking around me, stepped towards me and has poured into me? As our gazes meet, I realize—it's you.

You stayed? You stayed! You stayed when no one else would. A month, six months, a year...you stayed.

Even though it caused you to weep, and even though it meant sharing in pain or sorrow, you chose to stay when it would have been easier to run. You helped me to live again.

Many ask, "What can I do for you?" or "What do you need?"

Stay.

Choose to sit with me a while. It may be difficult at times, and it may hurt. But I can make it through this loss if you stick by my side.

So many who have loved and lost are left so alone. No one is willing to walk the path they are on with him or her. No one deems it worthy enough to extend that grace, that help in time of need.

Oh, dear friend. It is the most holy place.

It is a most treasured place. It's filled with rewards that only eternity holds. Jesus walked on this earth and sought the brokenhearted. He yearned to heal the sick. He saved the battered and extended his hand to the weak. Just as Christ did, so should we.

I know that in my tremendous pain and loss I needed the comfort of friends and family. I needed them to say, "I am coming, no matter what you tell me!" and then, friends to show up on my doorstep, often in tears.

I needed people willing to cry with me, to hurt with me. I needed the prayers of the saints, because my thoughts were a mess and my words insufficient. I needed scripture to be read over me, to be shared with me daily.

I needed my husband, and he needed me. But I also needed people to lift him up, encourage him, and support him.

I yearned for people to share with me about their love for Piper. I yearned to hear their hurts and pains, their joys and sorrows. I wanted to talk about Piper, knowing others loved her too. I wanted people to ask why I have "Piper Kay" tattooed in pink on my left hand and what that means.

And praise be to God—He provided for our needs.

He decided to use the lady in the photo department at Wal-Mart who was bold enough to ask if the birth announcements I had printed were of my baby girl. She leaned over the counter and said, "Tell me about her." So I stood in Wal-Mart and shared the God-breathed story of Piper Kay.

He used the lady from James Avery Jewelry who was bold

enough to ask what the date meant when I got Piper's name engraved on a necklace.

And he used the lady at the grocery store who was curious enough to gently ask why my husband had 7-27-2011 tattooed on the top of his wrist.

All these were random, curious, and caring people who extended interest in the lives of someone they didn't know—and it brought a God-inspired piece of comfort and healing to us every time.

How much more should we who do life together and claim friendship with one another check up and show care in times of need? And yet, we are often so concerned about how we might sound, or are unsure of what to say, that too often, we just don't say anything at all.

A friend once told me, "I'm nervous—not nervous about you…more nervous that I will say something stupid or make things worse."

I implore you, don't worry about what you say! Sit with me, talk with me, and you will find that although you may be nervous, it will be okay. I need you more than you know, and you don't have to have it all figured out. I don't. Please, don't be silent!

Unfortunately, there are some who are left in alone the darkness during a time of tragedy. Their family may not rally, or their friends may flee. Please don't be one who flees.

I want to stay—for you, for others. Oh, may my heart never again be hardened to the brokenness around me. May the fear of not knowing what to say or how to say it never hinder me from pouring out love, however awkward it might be.

I yearn to be the one that someday, you who have been wounded look up and say—"It's you! And you stayed."

Stay, will you?

Chapter Five

On the Rock

"Sing a new song of praise to him; play skillfully on the harp, and sing with joy. For the word of the LORD holds true, and we can trust everything he does," Psalm 33:3-4 (NLT).

You always hear stories about how Zacchaeus was a wee little man or how Jesus walked on the water. And you often hear people use cliché statements like, "walking by faith not by sight," or "what would Jesus do?"

In this world around us it's not unusual to have someone pat you on the back and say, "I'm praying for you." And it is not uncommon to bow your heads at the dinner table and say a prayer. Most of the time it's okay to encourage someone by saying, "Just give it to God. He knows best." And although these statements, stories, and attempts at encouragement are part of our "okayed" culture, I have to ask—how much do you really believe what you are saying?

My mind keeps rolling over and over an image of me in the middle of the ocean, alone and frightened. There is a storm. A rainy, gray sky. Crashing waves. Howling wind. From my point of view, in the midst of this storm, I see nothing but choppy waters and pelting raindrops. I feel nothing but the coldness of water tossing me and the furious wind nipping at my face.

But as I tread water and turn around, there ahead of me is a massive boulder sticking out of the vast ocean. Can I swim any longer? Can I make it there? My body aches, and my muscles are tense from the ice cold water.

The waves make it difficult to move. They push me to the right, then to the left. I sob as I give my last attempt to reach the rock before I just give up and drown. My energy is spent, and I start to sob as I dive under the waves one last time. As I come up for air and spit out the water that has begun to fill my lungs, I let out a heart-wrenching cry. My tears join the rain that falls.

But as I look up to the sky and wonder "why?" I see the rock, just inches from my face, and my foot hits its foundation. The waves continue to beat around me and the wind continues to howl. Yet I cling to this rock and let out a sigh of relief—and it holds me safe.

"On Christ the solid rock I stand, all other ground is sinking sand..." I'm glad we can sing that while standing in church. But honestly?

Often I'm not standing on the rock. I am barely hanging on. I am clinging to the Rock in the midst of this immense storm, hoping that another gust does not come and knock my grip free.

We stand in church so often and sing these songs. We praise him, for he is worthy. Yes, he is! But—do we mean the words that come out of our mouths? Can I honestly say that I am standing on Christ, the Solid Rock? I'd have to modify it to "On Christ the solid rock I cling!"

What we truly believe is challenged when a storm hits.

I can say that through the experience with Piper, my beliefs were challenged, and I now know my God in a way that I never knew I could. He has blanketed Dave and me with peace that is impossible to have in the midst of death—apart from Christ that is. He has comforted us to depths that we did not know existed.

He has calmed us in the midst of complete anxiety. Why? Because God is true to his word!

He is who he says he is.

He is the "I am."

And when he says something, he means it! He will follow through. He will provide. He will be who he claims to be. Oh, what a security blanket to pull over our heads and hide under when the terrors of the night strike!

After we found out we had lost Piper, the first thing that came to my heart was the chorus, "He gives and takes away. But my heart will choose to say, 'Blessed be the name of the Lord[1].'" He gives, and he takes away. It is in the Bible[2]! But do we really believe this part of scripture?

So many people ask me why Piper is gone. Why is she not safe in my arms, and why, after carrying her nine months, did he call her home?

I've asked the same things.

Yet I know in full confidence that he had her days numbered. They were written in his Book of Life[3]. And how do I know that? He said it.

And why did he take her away? Because he is God, and we are not.

His thoughts are so much higher than our thoughts. His plans are so much greater than ours can ever be[4]. He said it, and I believe it. I believe with my entire being that he has plans for me that are so much greater than my pain and hurt!

I know that he will use Piper Kay Brawner through her death. I also believe, without question, that he will use her story to bring salvation to others. Why?

Because I know that my God is a good God[5].

---

1   Song by Matt Redman
2   Job 1:21
3   Psalm 139:16
4   Isaiah 55:9
5   Psalm 84:11; James 1:17

He is a good Father. He does not give us a stone instead of a loaf of bread[6]. If Dave, an imperfect sinful father, can wish the best in life for Adia, how much more will our perfect and Holy Father dream and wish for us as his children?

It is true! His word is truth[7]!

And I believe it. Although feelings may tell me to act and believe otherwise, my heart will choose to say, "Blessed be the name of the Lord."

"But Piper is gone," some would argue. "She is buried. She is marked by death. How is that good, Julie? How?"

Well, my sweet friend, we live in a fallen, broken, messed-up world. Sin has entered, and now there is death. Do I believe that in the beginning of time, before Eve bit into the forbidden fruit, God had planned to take Piper? Nope.

Did he foreknow and foresee it? Absolutely.

It didn't catch him off guard or surprise him. His plan is all encompassing. It is thought out in the mind of God himself, not some shabbily thrown together, spur of the moment "Plan B"—it is his masterpiece, his wonderfully orchestrated plan for our earthly lives[8].

For one thing, in the perfection of the beginning, there wasn't death. But before the entrance of sin into the world, God would have never dreamed to take a baby from its family. He does not desire to give me pain and affliction, tears and sorrow. We are his children too, so I know it must hurt his heart so deeply to see Dave and I shaken and broken from such tremendous loss.

He is a good God. He hates to see us hurt. But still…he is holy. And because sin entered the world by our doing, life cannot and will not be perfect. Life here on this earth cannot be pain free. We can attempt to sugarcoat it. We can think, in vain, that everything is going to be easy.

---

6   Matthew 7:9-11
7   John 17:17
8   Jeremiah 29:11-12

But God has a plan—he wants to see as many as possible return home to be with him[9].

We so often forget that he is in control, just like his disciples did when they hit a storm and their boat got a little rocky. We tend to forget that he is the ultimate source of life—he is the I AM.

In the midst of the thunder and rain, we must remember that he controls it all.

"They woke him up and said to him, 'Teacher, don't you care that we are about to die?' So he got up and rebuked the wind, and said to the sea, 'Be quiet! Calm down!' Then the wind stopped and it was calm," Mark 4:38-39 (NLT).

His ways are so much higher than ours. I have never attempted to understand the fullness of God's plan for me; it is impossible. He is GOD! I am...me! How could I even begin to imagine that I could understand his fullness?

Yet as I think about what has happened with the loss of Piper, I do not *understand* why she is not here. But I *know* why—because it will somehow further his kingdom through this tremendous heartbreak. Do I understand it all? Absolutely not. Will I ever this side of heaven? No. Do I trust him? Yes.

I trust him at his word.

I trust that if I am anxious and I give it to him, he will provide me with a peace that is beyond my understanding[10]. And I know that to be true, because he has done it. He has held us so tight and has wrapped us in his peace. He has filled every room of our home—wall to wall—with his peace.

I believe that I cannot lean on my own understanding, but rather I must trust in him with all my heart[11]. He will be faithful to make my path straight, day-by-day, and sometimes hour-by-hour.

I know that he had to look at the face of death when his own

---

9   2 Peter 3:9
10 Philippians 4:6-7
11 Proverbs 3:5-6

Son died, just as I had to with Piper. I know that his heart was broken, and it hurt him so badly, just like it did me. And I know that he had to be separated from his Son, Jesus Christ, for three days—which to him, probably seemed like a lifetime.

Yet I believe God is good. And although our definition of good may not couple well with pain, suffering, and loss—his definition does[12]. Why? Because in those moments, he holds us so tightly and shows himself so richly, that our lives here on earth are granted a small glimmer of the hope that is to come for eternity. And for that, I declare, he is good!

So I am clinging to the Rock—to the one who holds me in the midst of my storm. Some days, when the sun comes out, I feel the warmth against my skin. Other times, the wind beats so strong that my knuckles are swollen and bleeding from gripping so tightly.

It is then I realize that I am not standing on the Rock, and I cannot muster enough strength to pull my drenched body from the water and stand. But I will crawl back up there. And then, I will probably sit for a while—a long while. And eventually, I will stand again.

But through all these struggles my heart will choose to say, "Blessed be the name of the Lord."

In those moments of complete and utter darkness, it will be a choice I make—one that has no happy feelings attached to it. In those moments of warmth and sunshine it may be a much easier choice—and one with a few warm fuzzies. But no matter what my *feelings* are, I promise God one thing—I will always choose to bless His name.

"On Christ the solid Rock I cling.

All other ground is sinking sand.

All other ground is sinking sand."

---

12 2 Corinthians 1:3-6

Chapter Six

The Glass Box

"My thoughts are nothing like your thoughts," says the Lord. "And my ways are far beyond anything you could imagine. For just as the heavens are higher than the earth, so my ways are higher than your ways and my thoughts higher than your thoughts," Isaiah 55:8-9 (NLT).

Sometimes in life we feel so lost. What are we doing? Where are we going? What is this life really about? A few months ago my heart would have said, "What are we going to do with two little girls running around the house? How will I make it through basketball season carrying both Adia and Piper around with me?"

It only took moments for my viewpoint to change so drastically.

As I walk the streets of our neighborhood or drive around town, I feel as if I see life through a pair of unique spectacles that have altered my vision. I feel like I am standing on the outside a big glass box. Life is "normal" within the box. There is the hustle and bustle of daily routines. Work and deadlines create a brisk walk for most. There may be some pain and some hurt, but in contrast to those outside the box, it's quite minor.

As I stand on the outside the glass box—looking in—I realize that I now have a radically different vantage point. I am an outsider. I did not beg or bargain or dream for this view. It feels as if, only moments ago, I was hustling and bustling inside the glass box too. Now, as I stand here gazing in, my heart beats slower, my brain calms down, and time seems to be on my side.

My perspective has been altered forever.

The old spectacles that I once wore no longer correct my vision; rather they impede it. I need my new prescriptive lenses that I bought with such a high price, the price of losing my sweet baby Piper. With these new lenses in place, I realize that life is not how it appears.

When we really look, take the time to step back, and watch life exist around us, it should bring us to our knees.

God has a plan for our lives, and I don't want to miss it. I desire to walk wherever He leads. His footprints are there for me to follow, and I will choose to seize the moment and place my foot in the already imprinted sand and follow—closely.

"What if a tragedy like this had happened to me?"

I've had precious friends ask themselves this question—and you probably wonder that too. But find comfort in the truth that God promises to only give us what we can handle. He also promises to provide enough grace to get through it. So what if it happened to you?

I wish I could take this pain and heartache from every other woman. But God is in the business of changing lives, creating radical differences in our hearts and minds, and bringing glory to his great name. Therefore, things that aren't comfortable and are not normally happening inside the glass box will occur—but with the divine plan of creating individuals who will choose to leave everything else behind and follow Christ.

God desires to overwhelm us with his heart, his view, and his mission.

His heart yearns for us is to live beyond the walls of the glass box and to understand the depth of life, the truth of his vision, and the strength of his touch. Life is not something that just exists. It was created—by him.

Every day is a gift. Every breath is granted to us in hopes that we will look to the Creator and ask, "What do you desire to do with me today?" Our heartbeats are not our own. The blood that flows through each vein, even the breath that billows in our chest—it is not our own.

Does his Word not say that our bodies are the temples of the Holy Spirit? We do not belong to ourselves! His heart longs for the day when each one of us will realize that the moments we spend on this earth are not for us. Piper did not breathe one breath on this earth. And yet, we are granted numerous days—to honor him.

Every day of our lives—they are for him and for his glory.

But to offer our lives to be used by our Heavenly Father we must believe, ultimately, that he is God, and we are not the masters of our lives. We must believe that he has a plan for our lives and no matter the earthly cost, it will bring great eternal rewards. We must believe in heaven. We must claim truth. We must have faith.

For so long, these truths have resonated in my soul, but they seemed so abstract and unable to grasp. Now, taking a step outside the box that we humans have created, I see that it is not so hard to understand them after all.

When I say that I will follow him—no matter what the cost—I now know that price can be very, very high.

I know there's a price because, from an earthly perspective, our family has endured a tragedy that cost a life. Yet my heart truly sings, "No matter the cost, Lord, I will follow you." I have grasped the intangible. I have been granted the ability to stop life long enough to understand that I am no longer willing to hustle and bustle through these moments here on earth.

I do not want to allow my breath to escape from my mouth without purpose. I refuse to miss those precious moments with my child and my husband, or allow our family to be devoured by busyness and chaos. I will choose to believe in our God and take him at his word. And I will stay, following his footsteps in the sand, for as many days as I am granted on this earth.

"What if this happened to me?"

If you hold tight to the one who has created it all, I promise, you will remain. Christ never said, "If you follow me, life will be an easy road—so jump on board! Let's party!"

The scriptures are filled with heartache, tragedy, loss, pain, and suffering. Christ himself endured the ultimate of all of these—he hung on the cross. And not for anything he had done! Jesus died for *our* sins. Unfair? Yes! But our Christ sees it as grace. So why do we think we will live in this bubble and nothing will ever pinch us or prick us, and we will never be harmed?

Wake up and smell the fruit! Yeah, that forbidden fruit, those "apples" that we took a chomp out of so long ago; those "apples" that brought sin into the world. It was our fault! We humans just couldn't withstand temptation and pride. And because we took a bite of that juicy, red, nasty-tasting apple…death and destruction were brought into this world.

There are consequences to our actions.

There will be pain and suffering.

Those who followed most closely to Christ while he was here on earth endured their fair share of bruises, beatings, and pure suffering. But, they also knew Christ in a way that few did. They experienced the grace of God in a way that others will never know. They believed and clung to truth, unlike most. And because of that, they intimately knew this God who seems so distant to many of us.

Those who have suffered have taken a step outside the glass box and chosen to put on the spectacles that changed their lives forever.

In Matthew 4, Christ said to Peter, "Come, follow me, and I will show you how to fish for people." He is saying the same to you and I, "Sweet child, walk with me, and I will show you life in a way you never imagined you could see it. I will give you a vision from my own heart. I will use your very breath to impact this dark world around you. Come, follow me."

It is a calling that requires sacrifice. You have to leave the comfort of the glass box. Yet everything we know is inside that box! The hustle and bustle of every day is what has become familiar.

Oh, sweet friend, that which is unfamiliar…the waters that are unchartered? This is where Christ is standing, holding out his hand and asking us to walk on water with him.

He is not promising a life of waveless waters. He is not promising a path that is easy to walk. But Christ himself *did* make many promises and because of that we don't have to fear those choppy waters that he may call us to. And the rewards are great.

> "Blessed are the poor in spirit, for theirs is the kingdom of heaven. Blessed are those who mourn, for they will be comforted. Blessed are the meek, for they will inherit the earth. Blessed are those who hunger and thirst for righteousness, for they will be filled. Blessed are the merciful, for they will be shown mercy. Blessed are the pure in heart, for they will see God. Blessed are the peacemakers, for they will be called children of God. Blessed are those who are persecuted because of righteousness, for theirs is the kingdom of heaven. Blessed are you when people insult you, persecute you and falsely say all kinds of evil against you because of me. Rejoice and be glad, because great is your reward in heaven, for in the same way they persecuted the prophets who were before you," Matthew 5:3-12 (NIV).

Christ promises to walk with us and to carry our burdens for us. He promises to be our help in time of need, to provide grace that is sufficient, and to bless us in the midst of anguish and pain.

It may not be easy, this life we are called to. But the choice is yours.

You can live life boxed up in the mundane or you can refuse to live within the confines of the glass walls, and you can see life through the eyes of our Savior.

Peter left his nets—immediately—and followed after Christ. How long will it take for you to leave your nets behind and run hard after the one who has saved you?

Life will be dramatically altered.

Your viewpoint will change.

But God is offering to give you spectacles that allow you to see from his vantage point. Trust me when I say—seeing clearly is exhilarating.

Chapter Seven

Hope in the Haunting Questions

"Who told us we'd be rescued? What has changed, and why should we be saved from nightmares? We're asking why this happens to us who have died to live? It's unfair."

—From the song "Held" recorded by Natalie Grant and written by Christa Wells

I've begun to realize that the complete emotional and physical exhaustion I experienced is partly due to the tremendous volume of questions and answers I have had to find and to give—to others and to my own heart. When the doctor looked at me with such sorrow in her eyes that day, the nightmare became a reality, and with it came so many unanswered questions, so many demanding decisions, and so much pain.

When you birth a baby, all you really have to decide is if you want the epidural (YES!) and how many nights you will stay in the hospital. Yes, there are decisions to make when you get that baby home. But they are joyous decisions, ones that come with coos and giggles, drool and diapers.

My questions had to be asked—and answered—in the midst of overwhelming grief.

While every situation is different, every loss is nonetheless heart wrenching. Whether you have lost a child, a spouse, a sibling, or a friend—it cuts deep into your soul, and there is emptiness that now becomes your reality.

Mental exhaustion sets in. Questions flood your mind, and if you read about the stages of grief, you know you'll be a little fuzzy. Yes, yes, you will! Why? Because your brain is going a million miles an hour, and answers to the questions you have are not easy to find. You are trying to process that which is outside your realm of understanding.

Physical exhaustion sets in—from your body working so hard, from your stomach convulsing as you sob, and from your tear ducts pouring out all you have within them. You ache with an ache that is overwhelming.

But decisions must be made. Questions must be answered. For us, the questions began immediately. And we had to find strength, confidence, and hope within the answers.

Do you want to wait to go into labor naturally or be induced? Uh—with a panicked, sorrowful look on my face, I said, "We want to induce!" I'm not even sure if I could have requested a C-section. At that moment, I was thinking about so many things that requesting to be cut open was not one of them.

They had to schedule a time for me to be induced in the hospital, and thankfully we could do it that next morning. *But why not right then?* I remember thinking, *Let's get me in the hospital ASAP and get this over with!*

I know that as painful as it was for me, the hospital had to work out the details on their end and have the correct staffing to deal with the birth of a stillborn. They had a few nurses that were specifically designated to tending to our family's needs. They had contacted the hospital benevolence volunteers who had gifted a handmade precious white dress, bonnet, and booties for our Piper Kay. They had prepared a place for her in the nursery. They were ready.

Looking back, I am so glad that we had that last night to

have Piper and those few extra hours to sleep with her, to cry with her, and to prepare for the moments, and the hours, and the days ahead. I am also glad that we chose to induce. I didn't know much about stillborns and I didn't know that the longer Piper stayed in my tummy, the more her skin and lifeless body would deteriorate.

Do we hold her? No! No way! That is crazy! My heart was already broken. Even the *thought* of holding her seemed too much to bear.

Do we take pictures? No!

Do we bring Adia up there to see her sister? No!

All the "No!" answers to these hard, hard questions came immediately, spontaneously, and out of hearts filled with pain. But God held our hearts tenderly and whispered to us, "She is yours. She is your child."

Yes. Yes. Upon hearing God's tender and loving words, our answers to these questions immediately changed from a solid "No" to a calm and loving "Yes". God's love and comfort and care had changed our hearts in the midst of such overwhelming tragedy.

Yes, Lord. Yes.

We held her.

We kissed her.

She was wrapped in a beautiful hand-made white blanket. We saw her fingers and her toes. We realized she looked just like Dave—same eyes, same nose, same long arms and legs.

We took pictures.

As we held our baby girl, Carol Howard quietly stood back, at a distance, and took pictures. She was from Now I Lay Me Down to Sleep Ministries, and Carol donated part of her life to capture the special moments we had with Piper Kay here on earth. We would not trade those precious black and white photos for anything. They are truly a treasure.

Adia met Piper.

Adia joined us in the hospital after Piper was born. She sat with us and held her baby sister. She pointed to her sister, "Eyes! Nose! Mouth!" Adia had the most beautiful smile, captivated by the beauty of the little baby she was holding.

We whispered in Adia's ear, "This is your sister—Piper." Adia treasured that day; I know she did even though she had just turned two a few weeks earlier. She was overjoyed, and the look on her face lit up as she touched her baby sister and investigated the little hands and feet. Still to this day, she looks at the picture of the four of us that is hanging in the hallway and says, "Baby Piper!" She remembers. And every time we say, "Yes sweetie. Piper is your sister."

As Piper was taken away, Adia screamed a piercing, haunting scream that brought immediate tears to my eyes and broke me to the depths of my heart—"NO! Baby!! No! I want! I want baby!" She didn't want to let go of her sister. She felt everything we felt, and she expressed it so perfectly—with childlike innocence.

Do we have a funeral? Do we bury her? What do we do?

I was going to have this baby, but she wouldn't be coming home. Dave and I were going to the hospital, and we didn't know how it all was going to work. What on earth do we do with the body?

My initial reaction was to not have a funeral because I didn't want people to feel obligated to come. It hurt too much.

This loss was a huge tragedy. It pierced not only our souls, but also the souls of so many people. Piper was due to join us here on earth. She had been functioning just fine in my belly only days before.

And now—death.

As we talked through answering this question, we decided to have a funeral. Thankfully, Dave's mom and dad jumped in to make all the arrangements. I knew Dave's mom was on the phone making many of the plans for us, and we were so grateful that she was taking care of it.

Dave and I didn't know what decisions we even had to make! We didn't know what questions to ask or even what to think. Our heads were spinning in clouds of thick pain-filled fog.

But Dave's mom did it for us. She would talk to the funeral home, and then she would bring everything to us, patiently explain it, and gently let us choose.

Do we ask for an autopsy?

We decided not to do this. She was perfect. We trusted completely in the arms of our Heavenly Father and knew that without a doubt, he had called her home. In Piper's case, there was no cord wrapped during delivery and there had been no signs of any problems during pregnancy.

There would be no answers, and we were okay with that. The placenta was tested and found to be normal. There were no complications in our situation. There had been no signs of anything wrong. And that is why we knew—it was God's ultimate plan, and there was no need for an autopsy in *our* case.

Her body was taken from the hospital by a funeral home. I can't imagine how Dave must have felt when he had to sign off on the paperwork that day in the hospital.

Embalming?

For us, we checked the "No" box. We wanted to embrace the memories of beauty we saw that day in the hospital. As Dave signed the papers to release her body, just like that, she was gone—forever. Her body was transferred to the funeral home. Then we had to decide…

Where do we bury her?

We decided to bury her in the beautiful hill country in New Braunfels. The grave faces the rolling hills that we love so dearly, where Dave was raised, and the place he calls home. So that is where we chose to place her precious, tiny body—at Hill Country Memorial Gardens in New Braunfels, Texas.

43

As we left the hospital that dreadful evening, birthing a baby yet leaving without her, Dave grabbed my hand in agony. The nurses kindly waited to release me until the other women in the birthing unit had cleared out. They waited because they knew we would be leaving empty handed. We walked that long hallway and realized—it was only the beginning. We were so sad, yet had so many decisions to still make.

The coffin?

Because we buried Piper in New Braunfels, we packed up our things and headed south. In the days following her death, we spent so much time planning her funeral. The first time we drove up to the funeral home, my eyes filled with tears. My heart ached. My stomach felt ill. We walked through the long halls to the meeting room. Answering questions about the death of your child isn't something anyone dreams of.

"What coffin do you want for Piper?" As we looked at the one that was free of charge, our hearts sank as we visualized her little body inside. It had a cheap button to hold the top somewhat closed. As Dave's mother looked at it, she asked, "Is there another?"

The man pulled out another casket, a shiny, bright, white one for the purity of our baby girl. It was so tiny. So perfect.

Then it struck me—I knew that somewhere in that building laid the body of my daughter. Her lifeless form was there, somewhere.

I remember yearning to see her, wishing somehow this could be like a Disney movie, and by bathing her in my tears, she would come back to us. But reality stood before me—in the form of a tiny coffin.

The shiny, bright coffin had a seal. It would keep her precious little body safe in the ground that she would soon be laid in. It was white and beautiful. It was now hers.

Then we went to the flower shop, and as we stepped to the back of the shop, we could barely speak a word. We saw the lady hand making our daughter's flowers. Pink Gerber-daisies were intertwined in beauty. They were perfect. But it broke our hearts.

How much more could we handle?

Is this not enough?

Planning the funeral for your child—the baby that should be in your arms—what other questions are there to answer? I have learned that the rest our lives will be filled with an array of questions about Piper and that we will have to choose to answer them, each with all the faith and hope we can muster.

Do we get her a headstone?

For us, the answer was unequivocally yes. And not only a headstone, but the best one we could find. We decided on a headstone with her picture engraved on the stone. We chose our favorite picture of Piper and had it perfectly engraved on a granite stone. It says, "Piper Kay Brawner; July 27, 2011; Longing to hold you again." We decorated around it beautifully, with the most pink as we could. And as the years go by, we will continue to put our best effort into making Piper's grave the most beautiful one that it can be. She deserves nothing less.

Do we go out to her grave—the first night after the funeral?

Yes. As her loving mother, I could not bear the thought of her body lying there just covered with dirt...all alone. So Dave and I went out there that first night. We took a pink and green cross to her grave, and it had a butterfly on it in memory of the service. We hung it over her headstone, on a hook that stands a few feet out of the ground. We even covered the wire that held the cross with pretty pink tulle.

We placed flowers on her grave, but we knew they would quickly wilt in the summer heat. So we also placed a plastic solar bush with bright pink buds there, sitting in a green pot filled with gorgeous stones to hold it firmly in the ground. We knew this solar powered bush would soak up the sun during the day, and shine over her all night.

A pink pinwheel also stands there, blowing in the breeze. It was a perfect gift to us from a friend of Dave's parents. It was given to us the day of the funeral, and it remains a lovely addition for Piper's grave. A matching pinwheel spins daily in our front garden at our home. The other day, a friend visited her grave—to stop by to talk to God about Piper. I smiled when she shared that it is the happiest grave she had ever seen. That is our testimony of Piper Kay.

What do we do with her room?

Do we pack it all up? Do I get rid of things? Where do we put it all? It is set up, ready and waiting for her to come home—but she's not.

Friends rallied around, pushed me into the kitchen and said, "We got this, Jules. We got this." They gently, preciously, carefully took every article of clothing, every toy, and every wall hanging—and packed it all in boxes for Dave and me to take to storage.

They compassionately took the boxes of diapers back to the stores and tried their best to get full store credit. They were assertive, yet gentle. And this was the perfect combination of what we needed.

We transformed the room from a baby room to a spare bedroom. Will that change the memories? Oh no. But it helped ease the pain—just a smidgeon.

But questions still continued to haunt me.

Do I go back to work?

I didn't have a baby to take care of, so I tried to say, "Yes." Yet I think that, depending on where you work and what surroundings you are in, the answer to this question will vary from person to person.

As I attempted to walk through a week of teacher in-service, getting ready for the 2011-2012 school year to begin,

I was completely overwhelmed. I felt that, in the busyness of preparing for school and teaching math to fifth graders, I had been forced to suppress the thoughts and memories of Piper. It had not even been a month yet. So I had to sit back and ask myself, *Do I start Monday morning with the kids here? Can I handle it? Will I explode with an ungrateful kid and tell them—AT LEAST YOU'RE BREATHING!!!*

Do I quit? Do I take a leave of absence?

I was exhausted from an entire week of pondering these thoughts. So in defeat and embarrassment, I walked into my doctor's office the next Monday to have her fill out my FMLA paperwork. *How can I rightfully take a leave?* I thought. *I can't check the box here that says, "Birthing and taking care of one's child." I don't have a living child to care for! How embarrassing it would be for me to take a leave of absence and have nothing to show for it!*

Yet as I walked through the door to the doctor's office, I was greeted with such tender compassion from my nurse. "Girl, the doctor will give you whatever time you need off! You need six weeks? Three months? Six months?"

Through tears, the nurse sat with me as she looked at pictures of Piper that I had brought to show them. She reassured me that there should be no embarrassment. This is something that not many face, she told me. And she comforted me as she explained that although situations are different for everyone, anyone who experiences a loss needs time to grieve and recover.

She shared with me that there had not been a day since July 26 that the office staff had not been thinking about us. Our tragedy hit their entire doctor's office with as much shock as it did us. The answer to "Do I take my leave of absence?" Absolutely.

Though each of us may handle grief differently, I suggest you strongly consider taking some time off, if it's an option for you. As psychologists tell us, if you don't deal with your grief and loss, the pain, the grief, the heartache will eventually come back to haunt you. And although it was painful and difficult, I'm glad I took the time to begin to digest it all then. I thought that time alone with my thoughts would be harmful. Rather, it was a welcome time to begin healing.

Do we send out birth announcements?

Having some time on my hands now, I continued taking Adia to her school, so I got lots of things done. I filed paperwork; I replied to emails; and then we answered this next question. I would send announcements.

I got online, and I created an announcement with a little pink butterfly. I wrote a thank you to all who had been praying for us. In the announcement, I shared that although we lost Piper, we can't wait to see her again.

I printed them at Wal-Mart, and I printed a ton of them. As I addressed the envelopes, I cried and I rejoiced. I am so proud of my daughter. She is beautiful. And I am so thankful for the prayers that lifted us up during this terrible time.

I knew that over the next year, people would begin to forget about what happened to our family. But maybe, just maybe, with this card on their fridge, they'd see it and remember to pray for us. And that alone, I decided, would be worth sending the announcements out to everyone I could think of. We had many people thank us for sending an announcement to them.

Do I put pictures of her up?

For us in our home, that decision was easy. Yes! We want to remember Piper Kay Brawner. She is our daughter. And although there were many pictures to choose from, we selected those that showed the joyful moments of that fateful day.

We enlarged the picture of Dave, Adia, and me holding Piper. We enlarged the joyful picture of Adia releasing the butterflies that morning at her sister's funeral. Another beautiful picture of Piper that Dave and I just love is one where you can see that she looks just like him. We framed these and placed them around our home as a daily reminder. And the beauty of our two daughters forever surrounds us.

Do we talk about Piper with Adia?

All the time! Sometimes we get choked up and pause. But we will always share the memory of her sister. When we had the funeral for Piper, we got a matching solar bush and pinwheel for our front yard, and every day that Adia plays outside, we remind her—that's for Piper.

How will I sleep at night? How will I function during the day? How are we going to make it?

All these questions and so many more are a daily part of our lives. We will continue to wrestle with them, one by one, until the day we figure out all the answers—if we ever do.

For now, we know that every night we will lay our head on our pillows and hope that Adia sleeps through the night and wakes up the next morning. If we didn't have her in the other room, I'm sure it would be much, much harder! But we do have Adia, and we are blessed to have her.

So for now, we will hope for sleep and pray for God's army of angels to surround our house. We will beg the Lord to send his angels concerning us, to guard us in all our ways. We will petition him to lift us up. And when morning comes, we will tell ourselves to get up, get ready, and keep on breathing.

Some days will be better than others. But for now, I know that there is a lifetime ahead that will be swarming with questions to answer. There will be decisions that will always have to be made.

In the midst of it all, I know that his hand holds us, his peace comforts us, and he will send help to us in time of need. Praise be to our great and wonderful God!

Chapter Eight

A Jewel in Your Crown

"The nations will see your righteousness. World leaders will be blinded by your glory. And you will be given a new name by the LORD's own mouth. The LORD will hold you in his hand for all to see—a splendid crown in the hand of God," Isaiah 62:2-3 (NLT).

I wish I could sit with every person who has touched my life through this time and share the story of Piper. I wish I could pull out the pictures, watch the slideshow we made, answer their questions, and cry with them. I think they deserve that. But I know, in all reality, that's impossible. It will never happen.

I wish they knew how we were blessed by their touch. I wish they knew how honored we were to call them friends. I wish they knew. Yet I have to hold to the hope that someday, the Lord will honor them with a jewel in their crown—a jewel in the shape of a "P"—so they will know and always remember how they blessed us during this time without our Piper.

When the shepherds and wise men visited Christ in the stable, the scripture says that Mary treasured in her heart the things they said. It may be a mom thing; I'm not sure. But through the mourning and loss, we have been blessed and held, and I have treasured many things in my heart.

For Dave and me, life changed drastically that July 26, and we realized our home was forever changed. We had three bedrooms: one for us, one for Adia, and one for Piper. How quickly life turns from one direction to another. Our zombie-like bodies made it through the days only because we had to. But, throughout those days God also gave us moments that brought glimmers of hope and turned the corners of our mouths into smiles.

So many blessed us and stepped up and out of their comfort zone to pour out compassion.

The fact that Dave's family embraced the task of taking care of all funeral preparations was phenomenal. The world's longest but sweetest obituary was creatively written; the pink and white funeral was planned; and we felt that our baby girl was well taken care of.

They knew. They knew that we couldn't handle it.

They knew that we needed so badly to spend time holding, cuddling, laughing, and playing with Adia. They just knew.

I'm sure it was very difficult for them to make decisions about their granddaughter of whom they were hoping to meet. From releasing the butterflies, to inviting the attendees to wear pink and white to the funeral, joy as well as sorrow oozed from each person that Monday in the beautiful Texas hill country—because they knew.

And just as Dave's family took hold of the funeral arrangements, my family took hold of our home front.

The week previous, we had moved into a townhome so the girls would have a yard to play in. My mom and her friend had come up a few days earlier and helped do a quick set-up of the home. Although our walls were decorated and rooms set up, there was little-to-nothing in our pantry and no washer and dryer. So after we lost Piper, my family undertook caring for our home front. They filled the pantry with food and shopped for a washer and dryer so that when we came home after the funeral, our house would be as complete as possible.

I am most positive that a jewel for their heavenly crown will be waiting for them in heaven—they who so faithfully carried our burden when our shoulders were weak and when our hearts were broken.

We needed them.

On that hot, summer morning of the funeral, it meant the world to us that so many people would choose to take time out of their busy lives to faithfully line the drive of the cemetery to grieve with us, and to celebrate the life and death of our Piper Kay.

So many people rallied on our behalf.

There were precious friends from out of town who showed up at our doorsteps just hours after receiving the call from us. I told them, "Don't come…it's okay." They didn't listen. They just packed up their car along with their tears. They came, and they embraced us on our doorstep.

What a treasure—

To have friends who refuse to listen to our "it's okays"—because they love us so much.

To have a sister-in-law who stopped everything, chose to take off the entire next week of work, and stayed with us.

To have a friend pack her bag and say, "I'm in this for the long haul!"—and actually stay—taking care of our precious Adia with the utmost love and care.

To have another friend who would lay on the bed with Dave and me, compassionately hold us, and weep with us—a treasure beyond words.

To have family who immediately began to think about the details of the delivery, setting up pictures, or writing the obituary—we will never forget.

To have friends who were close before but have now become our permanently adopted brothers and sisters—because of the sorrow we shared. We no longer see them in the same light. We've drawn them closer to us, holding them with love and forever saying, "Thank you" for the part they played in our tragedy—and our healing. And although we do not share the same blood, we claim them as family. We will walk through life with them as our sisters and brothers.

They have become family.

All these people rallied around us, rallied for us, and rallied with us. And I believe that their "Piper-jewel" awaits them upon their heavenly arrival!

There are so many things that stick out in my mind, so many things that have touched us dearly, and so many little things that made all the difference.

Immediately, people began bringing food for us to eat, and with all our "rallyers," it was a good thing they brought food! We needed to feed so many mouths!

Others sent gift cards to our favorite grab-and-go food places.

We had friends say, "We want to come visit," and they actually came—for lunch, for a chat, for a play date with Adia. And it meant the world to us that people would take the time to travel to our home just to sit with us. People sacrificed their time to simply eat lunch with us, and it helped to take away a little bit of the ache.

One precious friend engraved a necklace and gave it to me so I could wear it close to my heart. A sign was painted for us that said, "A sister is a gift to the heart, a friend to the spirit, a golden thread to the meaning of life" with Adia and Piper's name on it together. It honored me so much because it acknowledged both of my daughters: my Adia *and* my Piper.

Dave and I wanted to keep Piper's name close to us always, so we both got tattoos. These tattoos have proven to be a true source of comfort to our souls. Having Piper Kay's name on the underside of our wrist helps us remember all the joys—and sorrows—of our journey with her.

We received so many cards, emails, and text messages.

The cards were so encouraging, and to know that our mailbox

was almost always full was a comfort to us. It meant that others were thinking of us and praying for us, and we both knew we needed as much prayer support as possible!

I would pour out my aching heart via email to precious friends, and they would read my emails and encourage me to keep on writing—not only because they wanted to hear from me, but also because they cared. Their concern kept me from feeling like a lunatic, and it meant a lot.

So many sent text messages that required no reply—just a simple, "I wanted you to know, I'm still praying for you". Those simple messages kept us going.

I had a dear friend who took the time to faithfully text me a Bible verse every day—even if it was closing in on midnight. I just knew she would somehow get to her phone before the clock struck twelve and send me something that our Lord had spoken to her, for me, through his Word. What a gift!

So many people asked how we were—even though I might say "awful"—and it was a great source of strength. I so appreciated that there were certain friends who would always ask, even though it may have been awkward for them. They chose to stick their necks out and stay with us through the pain.

Many gave money to help us financially as well as to support the Piper Kay Memorial Fund at Deer Creek Camp. Knowing that people would give their hard earned money so that a child could go to camp in Piper's place to hear about Jesus was a cherished and humbling sign that she was—and we were—loved.

The coworkers at my school surprised us by planting a tree in a nearby park in honor of Piper. As Dave and I sat at the tree planting ceremony, a kids' choir sang. One child was the most joyous little red-headed girl, and I couldn't help but think that Piper would have been just like that joyful little girl. We both knew, and it made us cry.

Piper would have been that little spice-ball, right next to her sister, singing her heart out in joyous celebration.

Since we live four hours from her little grave in New Braunfels, it was a precious thought and a sweet gift to plant a tree just a few miles from our front door. At Thompson Memorial Park in Waxahachie, Texas, there is a precious baby Chinese Pistache planted in honor of our Piper Kay. We take Adia there often to play in the park, to hug the tree, to smile a sweet smile, and even to endure a little sadness, knowing that Piper isn't here with us.

One morning, a few weeks after we lost Piper, Dave woke up and did his daily skim over one of his favorite basketball websites. He was quickly overwhelmed to see a pink banner that had been inserted across the top of the website with his daughter's name. The website is a coach's forum. They had heard of the loss that we had endured and had taken the initiative to collect donations for a fund in honor of "Piper Kay Brawner" and her family. We were overwhelmed with humble gratitude for such a generous outpouring of kindness from people we have never met.

And then, one day, another sweet friend called to gift one of the greatest treasures of all!

In memory of Piper, the Barner family raised enough money to build a well in Uganda. This well would provide clean drinking water for an African community and forevermore be a promise of hope—in memorial of the death of Piper. The ministry of Holden Uganda builds wells that reach between 500 and 2,000 Ugandan people—and each well is dedicated to a baby or a child who has gone to heaven before their parents.

Piper Kay Brawner is now a part of ministering to others—by providing physical water and by spreading the hope of Jesus Christ, our living water.

Wow!

All of these many friends and family have touched our lives deeply. They have ministered to us in many different ways. As each has reached out to us in our brokenness, they were the hands and feet of Jesus himself! It has meant so much to know that in the midst of our tremendous pain and heartache, people chose to hurt with us. And knowing that those around us hurt too, knowing that they miss Piper Kay, and knowing that they sometimes cry themselves to sleep—just like us—brings great comfort because we know we are not alone.

It shows the depths of love. It exhibits the beauty of friendship. It deepens the level of trust.

I'm so comforted that they all choose to walk with us, question and vent with us, and cry tears of joy and tears of pain with us as we journey together. I know they could easily choose to close their hearts and protect themselves from this pain. But, just like the friends in Mark chapter two, they were willing to carry our paralyzed family and remove the roof and lower us down before the feet of our Jesus. Just like those who carried the man to Jesus, our friends carried us in faith, knowing that we needed to sit before our God and be healed.

I know that there will be some who will follow the dates on the calendar and choose, again, to hurt with us as July 27 rolls around every year. Some may visit her grave. Others may send a card or email or text, because Piper has touched their lives so deeply—and because they care.

I hope there will be many who will continue to pray for us as they view the picture of our family on their fridge. I hope there will always be those who remember our little Piper, those who will remember how we lost a precious part of our family, and those who will never stop praying for us.

I am so thankful that God promises to provide for all our needs in so many different ways.

It may be in a painting or a necklace, a card or a hug. It may be a seemingly tiny little act of love or a huge sacrificial gift. All of them matter.

Most of these people will never know how special their time, their words, or their gifts have been. We may never be able to express how overwhelmed with gratitude we are to have their thoughts and prayers. But I truly believe that there will be a special jewel in heaven set aside for them. And as our Father places that pink and green gem in their heavenly crown, I believe he will look into their eyes, and say, "I tell you the truth, when you did these things for one who is heartbroken, wounded, and overwhelmed,—that someone was me! You did it to me!"

So often, when we come across someone who has lost a loved one, we do not know what to say or how to bless him or her. I know that my journey may be different than anyone else's—because each story is its own book. But I hope you now know that even in the smallest gestures or seemingly insignificant gifts, you plant a seed of hope and provide a glimmer of light.

You are storing for yourself treasures in heaven, my friend!

Chapter Nine

Our Love Through it All

"I don't get many things right the first time. In fact, I am told that a lot. Now I know all the wrong turns, the stumbles and falls brought me here. And where was I before the day that I first saw your lovely face? Now I see it every day. And I know that I am the luckiest."

—From the song "The Luckiest" written
and recorded by Ben Folds.

I'm in love. I married my best friend. Over the years, we have grown to depths of love that I didn't know was possible. I've learned about love and compassion and mercy through this marriage of ours. I've treasured the way he loves me, and I've attempted to be even half as good as he is to me!

It was *not* love at first sight. A friend of mine had a crush on this six-foot-tall guy. One day she pointed him out to me on the Texas A&M campus, and I told her, "He's *all* yours!"

Little did I know that his humor would lure me in, his witty comments would challenge me, and his passion for life would inspire me. Even Dave's shoulder-length hair and bold, plaid pants enticed me.

I was in love.

We studied together in college, laughed over the same subjects, and watched lots of movies. The first time he held my hand, I cried and told him we would have to end the relationship. I panicked. He calmly spoke wisdom over me, and as the years went on, he decided to make our relationship—forever.

He proposed—with a big elaborate plan.

We enjoyed a night of ice cream and a simple date. But we ended it on a quilt—in the middle of nowhere—with a picnic for a late night snack. He had mowed one circular patch—only enough for the blanket. And there I sat as he read some goofy poems that he had written.

He was the master of writing poems. In one that he wrote for that special night, he included a huge ring with the most beautiful blue "emerald" that was taped to the part of the story where the king asks the queen a question.

Was he trying to ask me to…? A king and a queen? Was he asking me to…?

I know I was shocked, but as he pulled the ring off the page, he leaned toward me and said, "Don't worry, baby. The ring isn't real."

Whew! The night continued with laughs and stargazing. Then my sweet, humorous, David Preston leaned over and asked me to be his—forever—and this time it was for real.

"Are you sure this ring is for real? I don't believe you now!" I said. It was real, and being avid Ben Folds fans, we chose for me to walk down the aisle toward my precious husband as the words of "The Luckiest" played for all to hear. Why?

Because we both feel as if we are the luckiest—the luckiest couple of all.

Over the years, our marriage has simply grown deeper, stronger, and richer. We share so much—large and small—the passion of putting up as many Christmas lights as possible in hopes "of annoying the neighbors"; wearing our matching Griswold Family Christmas T-shirts throughout the holidays; enjoying the challenge of finding the greatest deal on used clothes while thrift store shopping; purchasing our yearly poster board to map out our NCAA March Madness bracket as we follow the wins and losses of college basketball; traveling to the heights of the mountains in North Carolina to whitewater raft; or heading to the Caribbean and soaking in the sun.

There are simply so many things we enjoy together.

I love to watch Disney movies, so Dave patiently sits with me—although now with his iPhone on hand (I'm sure he can secretly stream something more entertaining on it as I finish watching my *Beauty and the Beast).*

Many of Dave's attributes I have craved to have as my own.

He has always led by example in his love for me. His unconditional love and patience have been a part of his character since the day we met. He has a heart for children and a desire to teach and coach that is inspirational to all who see it. Dave has a quietness of soul yet a strength of character that amazes me. As we pursue loving Jesus together, I truly believe he is a man after God's own heart. His name suits him perfectly, just like King David in the Old Testament. All this makes me desire to be godly, just as he proves it in the way he lives.

By doing life together, he has rubbed off on me. His influence and his love have helped mold me into the loving and compassionate person that I am. I am honored, and I know that I have been called to be his wife. Although I graduated with an Engineering degree from Texas A&M, I married my sweet husband and became the wife of a coach, witnessing his amazing love for kids—and I became a schoolteacher.

I know that I was created to live life with David Brawner. Our life together has been an interesting road, but I have enjoyed every bit of it—until now.

I just can't put losing Piper into the "enjoy" category. But what I would say is that, through this tragedy, I have experienced the depths of love—depths I never knew were possible in a marriage relationship. I look at my husband and am overwhelmed with love that I cannot explain nor express completely.

I treasure him.

What a man of God—to endure losing his baby girl, yet still be able to hold and comfort me. What a husband—to know that in the midst of his pain, he cries—because he desires to be with me and hold me and cherish me.

I have never doubted his love for me. Now? It is unmistakable.

It is written all over his face. When his blue eyes gaze into mine, I know—we are going to be okay, because we're walking it out—together.

In the midst of our loss, many people asked us, "Have you read the book, *Heaven is For Real*?" So Dave and I decided to read it together.

One night we were lying on the bed together, and I pulled out the book. I flipped to the chapter titled, "Two Sisters," and began reading, but tears filled both our eyes. There came a point where I had to stop reading before I could move on. It had reinforced what we already knew:

Piper is standing on the streets of gold and celebrating with Jesus Christ.

And as Dave and I continued to read about this other family who also had a daughter in heaven waiting for them, we smiled. We found a measure of comfort and peace in their story and in this truth:

Piper will be waiting for us.

But was this a terrible dream? Can we ever wake up from all this? Did we really lose our baby girl?

While Piper was with us on earth, we knew that she was a girl. We had named her, and her room was decorated in pink and green, ready for her to come home to. But she didn't come home, and we miss her—terribly.

I think about those times when Adia lays on the spare bed with me. She'll look up at me, and she says, "Mommy, baby?" It breaks my heart, for she knows there was supposed to be a baby in this room. As young as Adia is, she misses her sister too.

I know that Adia is a daddy's girl. She looks unmistakably like her father. She has his big blue eyes, his cute little nose, his broad shoulders…and is tall, long and lean. She has always been a perfect mold of him.

When we found out we were having another baby, I would tease Dave. Surely, our second child will look like me! But then, when Piper was born, we looked into the face of our daughter, and she looked just like…Dave! I couldn't believe it.

Piper's baby pictures next to Adia's? Identical. You would not be able to pick them apart.

That night when we were reading, I laughed out loud, brushed his head with my hand, and I told him, "Piper looks just like you, baby." He buried his head in my chest and let the tears flow. She was his baby girl too.

Being a daddy and having a daughter is something very special. Dave was supposed to teach Piper how to play basketball. He was going to twirl with her and dance with her. And someday, he would have walked her down the aisle, beaming with pride. Dave's heart broke the day we lost Piper in a way I've never seen before or since.

And his tears still flow—from a soul that has been pierced and wounded, a daddy's heart that wants so badly to hold and rock his baby girl.

I know that people see loss and immediately care for the woman, attempting to ease her pain. We women are emotional people, and losing a child hurts us deeply. I have hurt in ways I didn't know were possible.

But let us never forget that when looking death in the face, men are pierced to their depths as well.

Yes, they handle it very differently. At times, they may bottle it up. Some cannot bear to look at pictures of the loved ones they've lost; other cannot bring themselves to visit the grave.

Some fathers may not have been able to hold their baby, knowing that death was real. They shield their hearts from the pain and grief. They don't know what to do.

Although they are tough on the outside, there is pain and sorrow on the inside.

We all know that men and women are so very different. That is no shocker. But through losing Piper I have seen firsthand that men and women deal with grief and loss in such different and unique ways. It is important to stop, watch, and listen to the heartbeat of your man. When I did, I was given a glimpse into the painful depths of a father's heart, and that is very different from a mother's.

One night when Dave and I were sitting in the quietness of our home, it hit me that I will never see Piper get married. As I mentioned that to him with tears rolling down my cheeks, he could not meet my gaze and whispered, "I know. That was one of the first things that broke my heart. I will never get to walk her down the aisle or dance with her on her wedding day." At that moment I realized, although he hadn't been verbally speaking about every little thought, his heart was breaking silently, and his soul was mourning—just as deeply as mine was.

He just struggled to speak about it.

My challenge?

When his words are few, and he is silent, I need to be patient and wait for his heart's timing to be able to share with me.

When he has spurts of anger or frustration, I should respond with kindness and remember that he is struggling to process this loss, just as I am.

When he is filling his time with being busy or turning on the sports' channel when the house seems quiet, I have to remember that these things just might help him manage his loneliness.

I cannot think that the only right way to grieve is my way—through openly sharing and discussing our loss. That would be selfish, assuming that I am right and he is wrong. Rather I need to remember that we are both grieving the same loss—in different ways.

I need to honor him with patience, understanding, and grace, just as Christ has extended that to me. I must pray for his healing, trusting that God holds his heart. I must protect our marriage by praying fervently, and always persevere no matter the cost.

I know that there will be hard times. I know that there will be ups and downs, smiles and tears, anger and sorrow. Yet through it all, I need to remind myself that we are both processing the same loss in two very different ways—and we will journey this loss by walking in the footsteps of Christ's love.

I had to call my husband the other day and apologize for not praying for him enough. I pray for Adia like crazy. She is on my mind all the time, and I desire for her to be safe and grow in the goodness of our Father.

But I must never forget my sweet husband—the one whom I fell in love with so long ago.

I cannot forget to lift him up in prayer, to be patient with him as he copes with our loss as only a man does, and to pour out the tremendous love for Dave that God has granted me. Our days are numbered as well, just as Piper's were.

There is no way I'm missing out on time with my Dave. No way! I'm in love. I always will be. There will be no other like my Dave.

He is my man, and I am the luckiest.

> "Love is patient, love is kind. It does not envy, it does not boast, it is not proud. It does not dishonor others, it is not self-seeking, it is not easily angered, it keeps no record of wrongs. Love does not delight in evil but rejoices with the truth. It always protects, always trusts, always hopes, always perseveres," 1 Corinthians 13:4-7 (NIV).

Chapter Ten

Daddy's Girl

"So I will dance with Cinderella while she is here in my arms. 'Cause I know something the prince never knew. Oh I will dance with Cinderella, I don't want to miss even one song. 'Cause all too soon the clock will strike midnight—and she'll be gone."

—From the song "Cinderella," written and recorded by Steven Curtis Chapman

You know that there is a special piece of a father's heart that holds his baby girl. For some reason, God created a unique and precious bond between a daddy and daughter. Over the past two years, I have treasured this truth, watching that love unfold in the relationship between Adia Michele and her daddy.

She loves him so much. She looks just like him. She wants to follow in his big footsteps. She is his baby girl.

Dave and I had talked about our concerns of having room in our hearts for two precious girls. How would that be possible? We love Adia so much and are so proud of her! And when Piper Kay was born, the pride of a father seeing and holding his two daughters poured out from him in a mixture of intense pain and sorrow. We indeed had room enough for the two of them.

Dave internalizes his emotions, to say the least. He holds his feelings in for the most part. And he does a pretty good job of it. But this?

How does anyone really know how to cope with such pain?

How do you move forward in this life when you internalize things? This kind of grief you can't just leave un-mended. This kind of loss is something that needs to be surfaced and resurfaced and dealt with over the many years to come. We know this, and we will try to deal with our loss as we attempt to live life without Piper.

One night, I noticed that Dave had been journaling. And since we openly share everything, he offered to reveal his heart through his journal, giving me a glimpse of the deep pain he was truly in.

> "I'm sorry it's taken so long for me to write you, my little Piper Kay. I'm like all the other people who have no words for this kind of loss. My thoughts are a jumbled mess, and I feel like I'm here, watching myself go about my business day-by-day but not really living. I try to push my thoughts of you to the back, because I fear the floodgates are going to open. I love you, and I'm so sorry that I haven't written.

> Your life was but a vapor—poof and it was gone. But your impact is immeasurable. For nine months we waited, and honestly we wondered if we could handle another little girl. But we were ready and waiting. We were waiting for you, for you to appear. God had a different plan, though, and he knew that you were too beautiful for this earth, that your impact on us and others would be far greater if he just brought you home to him.

> For that I am jealous.

I am jealous that he gets to hold you. That he gets to see you dance, laugh, and play.

I am jealous that you won, that you finished the race first—and it's safe to say that, unlike you, I've just been crawling in this life so far.

But my sweet angel, I am so very happy for you.

I'm happy that you will never feel heart-wrenching pain like we felt when we had to give you up—or that you will never know betrayal or heartache. This is what I cling to, I take comfort in. You are, even now, in the presence of the Most High God, and he will never let you down like I undoubtedly would have.

You have left a hole in my heart that will never go away, that really, I never want to go away. No matter how long it takes me to get to you, I always want to feel that hole because it defines who I am now, and for it to be filled in would erase the fact that it happened. Yet I miss you, and I am only now starting to realize that you are not coming back.

Crazy. I must be.

I pushed you to the back of my mind when I went back to work, and I tried to suppress the emotion. But that is not fair to you or to me or to your mom. I'm sorry my angel.

I wish you could have known your mom. You would have figured out pretty quickly who got the better end of this marriage. This guy. I did!

She's an amazing woman, and she is going to share your story with the nations. She's the real warrior in this family.

I wonder if you would have been feisty like your mom and sister. I hope so.

I was really nervous about adding another girl to the family. I guess it is innate in us men to want a son, to think, "Of course we are going to have a boy." We want someone to mold into some sport's star—at least that's what I wanted. We men want somebody to do "man stuff" with, and we joke about our "man caves" and our wives' "time of the month stuff" that we know nothing about. But deep down, we men just feel more comfortable with a boy because that's who we are. We are beings with big brains, but most of that brain space is devoted to stuff we will never need—like Warren Moon's completion percentage or the secret codes to old Nintendo games.

The truth is—deep down we men are insecure about raising a girl, because we just don't understand you all the time.

So how would my imperfect parenting skills do the job of parenting—girls? I'm so unsure.

About a month before you went to be with your heavenly Dad, I had a change of heart about this. You see, I didn't so much care anymore about your gender; I was just excited to have you. In fact, I was even comfortable with the idea that you might be the last child in our family. Sure, I was a little nervous about the teenage years and then paying for two weddings, but it excited me as well. I couldn't wait to dance with you, to play HORSE with you, and hopefully to coach you—and to one day walk you down the aisle. I also got a little excited about embarrassing you when that first boy came over.

It's humbling to think of what your life has taught me, as short as it was.

You taught me to ask: how am I impacting the "eternal race"? You never know when your life is going to be significantly altered, so why waste time doing things that don't matter?

You have taught me the importance of family—of not letting your sister tug and tug on my leg until I finally respond, but engage with her quickly, and to play and not worry about what I want to do.

You have taught me the importance of loving the kids I coach and not worrying about the wins so much. Their eternity hangs in the balance, and I need to have an eternal perspective.

There are so many things that I wonder about, so many questions I have, but in the end, I just want to hold you.

> I love you baby girl.
> Daddy."

As I scrounged for Kleenexes, I also found a poem he wrote to Piper, just days after we buried her. A daddy's girl, forever she will be. He will always miss her. There will always be a part of him missing—until the day he can hold her again.

To My Piper

There's a hole in my heart,
Because of you, my little girl.
There's a hole in my heart,
Because I don't know if you have a curl.

There's a hole in my heart,
Because I won't see you with your sis.
There's a hole in my heart,
Because of all the life you will miss.

There's a hole in my heart,
Because we won't get to play HORSE.
There's a hole in my heart,
Because we won't ever get to the golf course.

There's a hole in my heart,
Because I won't get to walk you down the aisle.
There's a hole in my heart.
To see you again I'd crawl many a mile.

There's a whole in my heart,
Because of you, my little girl.

—Daddy

Chapter Eleven

Nine Months

"LORD, remind me how brief my time on earth
will be. Remind me that my days are numbered—
how fleeting my life is. You have made my life
no longer than the width of my hand. My entire
lifetime is just a moment to you; at best, each of us
is but a breath…and so, Lord, where do I put my
hope? My hope is in you," Psalm 39:4-7 (NLT).

I remember the night we found out I was pregnant with Piper.
I'm not sure why we tried the pregnancy test; we weren't
planning to have another baby so quickly. We had thought we
might wait till Adia was 5 or so before introducing a new sibling.
As the + sign became evident, I looked at Dave in horror and
yelled, "Go get a name brand one!! This is the store brand! I don't
trust it!"

He frantically ran out to get a new "name brand" pregnancy
test, and then, as he walked through the front door with it, we
looked at each other in disbelief. Is this really happening—now?
The answer to the second test? Two double lines: pregnant. I read
the instructions over and over, hoping I had read it wrong. Two
double lines: pregnant.

Welcome Piper Kay.

I was never one of those girls who, during pregnancy, gained no weight. With both Adia and Piper, I gained a full 50 pounds. My doctor was kind and never mentioned her concern. And everyone always said I "carried my weight" so well. Little did they know it was all stored in my hips and thighs!

There are some women who just love being pregnant. Not me! They make statements that sound so absurd to me. They loved it? They felt their best? They wish they could always be pregnant? What on earth are they talking about?

Me, on the other hand? After Adia, I never wanted to be pregnant again.

I teased my husband about this after my pregnancy with Adia. "Can we consider surrogacy?" Not that I was sick all the time or that I had complications with pregnancy. I just flat out hated it. I hated the tummy and the time when people didn't know if you were just fat or if you were actually pregnant. I hated the expansion of my hips and thighs. I hated the waddle that came to be all too familiar, and the feet that seemed to grow a few shoe sizes. I hated the back pain and the weight gain. And to top it off, I hated the sleepless, uncomfortable nights. I just didn't enjoy pregnancy.

I wanted more kids, but I dreaded the nine months it took to have them.

So after seeing the two double lines on that pregnancy test, we knew our lives would change. We knew our family was growing, and we were completely unprepared. We felt so insecure, so unready, so imperfect. We were terrified of bringing a second child into the world. And what if it was another girl?

As the days and months went by, our hearts grew to love this child. We began to dream of our future together, and I imagined taking the two little ones to basketball games to see their daddy coach. We had hopes that Adia and her sibling would play sports and play well together, loving one another and sharing in a passion for our Christ Jesus. We smiled as we thought about all the days they would share together—the laughter and the smiles.

When we found out we were having a healthy *girl*, we panicked nonetheless. But something happened that same day. When we learned we were adding our Piper Kay Brawner, our love grew to a size we didn't know was possible—and our smiles grew bigger and prouder than ever before.

We were going to be the parents of two little girls!

As I look back, I wish I had cherished those nine months more. I had nine months of holding Piper Kay in my tummy, and what did I do? Most of those months I spent complaining about how big my belly had gotten or how hard it was to walk around as I chased a two year old. I worried about my pant size being a maternity "large," and I wished I were smaller. I couldn't wait for those months to fly by and just be done with pregnancy, birth the child, and get on with life. I felt like those nine months were a holding pattern…useless and just there to take up time.

Oh, if I could just go back and redo those months—I'd treasure every moment.

Little did I know that in the midst of my complaining spirit, I was missing the only moments on this earth that I would share with my baby girl.

Those kicks at 2 a.m.? Those pant sizes that seemed to get bigger and bigger? Those tummy aches or days filled with morning sickness that seemed to last all day? If I could only have those moments back and in the middle of it all, sing instead of fuss.

I would take more time to read to Piper.

I would introduce Adia to her sister.

I would let her listen to more music.

I would rub her back, her hands, and her feet through my tummy—with extra love.

I would pray more over her and speak to her gently in the midst of the morning hours while I lay awake.

I would be excited to have a belly and be proud show off my growing tummy, rather than attempting to hide it.

I would be okay with people touching her, speaking to her, and blessing her.

I would…

If only we had known those were the only moments we would spend with her.

Dave and I both wish that we had done those nine months differently.

We wish we had reacted to that positive pregnancy test with joy rather than fear.

We wish we had taken more time to share our lives with her, together, through the womb that held her tight.

But we can't change any of that. There is no magic wand that can be waved to send us back in time. Therefore, we can only move forward. And as we move forward, we are reminded that we never know how many moments we have with the ones we love.

God has our days numbered.

We go through life thinking that our days will go on and on as we have planned. We keep thinking, *if we just keep moving, maybe we won't hit any bumps in the road.* But God never promised a narrow, smooth path in this life. He has called us, as believers, to walk down that narrow road. We don't know the length of our journey or how long he has called us to trudge through the dust and dirt of this world. But what we do know is that our life is fleeting and our days are numbered.

We must put our hope in our Lord and make every moment count for his glory.

And life counts! Whether you carry a child for nine seconds, nine minutes, nine hours, nine days, nine weeks, or nine months—it is your child. You begin to hope for things, plan for moments, and rejoice in the days ahead when you can hold your baby for the first time.

For some of us, those moments are ripped away. Those hopes

of a future with little newborn clothes and rattles are torn from us when we lose a child. And it hurts.

There are those who have been blessed to walk with their child for 9 years, 19 years, 29 years—and still, they are torn away from them all too soon. And this kind of loss is painful, no matter what.

We all know that it happens, but most of us hope that if we stay a healthy distance away from those who have lost, then maybe—just maybe—it won't happen to us. Yet God's plans are so much greater than ours. He holds us gently in his hands, and whispers, "Child—just hold on to today. I have given you this day. Live it to the fullest."

As I write those words, my heart aches. I wish I had chosen to cherish those moments with Piper just a little more than I did. But...

I know we loved on her.

I know she heard our laughter and our voices.

I know she felt her older sister climb and push and poke her.

I know she heard her sister's giggles.

I know we prayed for her.

But I crave to hold her now and watch her giggle with her sister now. I yearn to speak over her and sing to her now.

Someday.

Someday.

But for now, I cling to the truth that Jesus loves the little children, and I trust that, although we only had her for nine months, she knew our love and is now being loved by the ultimate lover—our Heavenly Father.

Chapter 12

We Promise

"It was there at Gilgal that Joshua piled up the twelve stones taken from the Jordan River.

"Then Joshua said to the Israelites, 'In the future your children will ask, 'What do these stones mean?' Then you can tell them, 'This is where the Israelites crossed the Jordan on dry ground.' For the LORD your God dried up the river right before your eyes, and he kept it dry until you were all across, just as he did at the Red Sea when he dried it up until we had all crossed over. He did this so all the nations of the earth might know that the LORD's hand is powerful, and so you might fear the LORD your God forever," Joshua 4:20-24 (NLT).

I've been dreading the thought of writing this chapter for a long time. I know that stories must come to an end, books must have a last chapter, and life will one day have its last moments before we pass into eternity. But the journey on this earth is not over—not until the day we meet Jesus face to face and we experience that perfect wholeness once again.

As we move forward in this life without Piper, I know there will be days of deep sadness. There will also be days filled with immense joy. Yet still, my heart will always wish that she were here to join in the celebration of laughter and happiness with us.

We will always be missing a part of us. We will always be without one member of our family. And we will always have a gravesite to visit. That will never change.

But our family will promise to always remember.

So often I think of those people who endure a tremendous loss like we have, but they attempt to hide their emotions. I think that their goal might be to bottle it up, to pretend it never happened, and to never talk about the life that seemed to be so unfairly ripped away. For them, it seems easier to just move on—as if nothing "hit the fan"—and they act as if everything is okay.

Is it?

I can honestly say that I firmly believe...we must remember.

If we, as mere humans, attempt to bottle up such huge pain, we might not make it through life! We might not succeed in keeping a lid on all that pain. And we may eventually blow up—to our regret. We become filled with more anger and pain than we would have had if we had walked through this journey of allowing ourselves to remember.

I've attempted both.

I've attempted to go on with life by bottling up the loss of Piper and trying—so hard—to move on, pushing thoughts of what happened to the back of my mind. By the end of that cycle, I fell harder and cried longer than if I had simply allowed myself to deal with the moment-by-moment pain and memories.

One night soon after her passing, as Dave and I talked about how this tragedy would impact our family, we made some promises.

We promised each other we would never forget our Piper Kay.

We promised to make an effort to visit her grave, even though we knew it would hurt terribly.

We promised to pursue teaching Adia about her baby sister, to teach her how to say "Piper", and to show her pictures of her sister.

We promised to talk about Piper with others and to share her story.

We promised to hang pictures in our classrooms and around our home—of both our daughters.

And if, someday, we are blessed with another living child…we promised that he or she will know about the sister who is waiting for us all in heaven.

We will remember.

We are so thankful for the pictures that were taken that day in the hospital. Life moves on so quickly, and it is often hard for us to hold on to the memories of lost ones. We know that someday, our memory will fail, and the face of our Piper Kay that is so visibly imprinted on our minds right now may fade. But we will hold dear to those pictures.

Others around us will forget. But we will not.

As July 27 rolls around every year, our family will take time to celebrate the memory of our precious daughter. And we know that God is at work here—through the memory of Piper Kay Brawner. I know it, I believe it, and I hold firm to the promise of our Father—that he is in control of it all.

So we will remember her life and her death, because in those moments I will be reminded that God is still at work.

The headstone we made for our baby girl has her picture on it. As we placed that stone on her grave, it was like Joshua 4, when Joshua had the people pile up the stones they had gathered from the Jordan. We who have lost a loved one pile up our own stones, not only in remembrance of those we have loved and lost, but also so we will never forget God's hand of help, even in those times of tremendous pain.

So we will pile our stones in remembrance of Piper Kay.

And when Adia asks why we visit this grave, why we bring

flowers, and why we pour out our love over this little plot of land that may seem like only a decorated pile of dirt, we will share with her:

"Because, we promised to remember."

We know that life must go on. But our lives are forever altered. Our lives will never be the same.

Almost everyone around us will continue to live his or her lives in normalcy, yet we who have loved and lost will limp along, wishing we could walk again without pain. It has become our reality, and we know Piper is never coming back.

There are days that I gaze at the picture on the mantel. I look at her sweet, tiny, perfect little face and think, *Surely this is all a dream! She was so perfect. She is perfect. If I could just hold her again, surely she would begin to breathe…* And then I have to step back, with tear-filled eyes and remind myself that this is my new reality.

Yet I praise God—for he did not leave us here, alone, in this darkness. I know that, in the midst of this pain, I will walk again! I may always have a limp or a slight swagger to my step.

But I will walk again.

That is the kind of Savior we have. Mark 1:30-31 tells us, "Simon's mother-in-law was lying down, sick with a fever, so they asked Jesus to help. He came and raised her up by gently taking her hand. Then the fever left her, and she began to serve them."

Jesus Christ simply took her hand. He gently touched her, and she was healed.

I know that he is holding me, and honestly, I feel like his grip at the moment is not very gentle, but rather it is firm and tight. My God has our family wrapped up tightly in his arms.

We know it. We feel it. We trust it.

And someday, as that grip loosens, he will set us down gently—and we will be healed. I believe that we will always have a mark of loss. How can we not? We will always be touched by the mark of death, but in a God-inspired way.

Our family has been chosen—to suffer.

Do I want to? No. Do we enjoy it? Um…not so much. Do we praise Him? Absolutely.

He has reached down and taken our Piper Kay from our family here on earth. He has her with him even now, praising and dancing and twirling. And why we can't twirl with her here and now is not for us to understand. We must trust that he will accomplish more for his kingdom through her death than would have been accomplished through her life.

For this reason I am certain that many souls will be touched by his love and healed for his glory through Piper's story of life— and death! The hand of the Living God has touched us—and we will not forget.

We promise to remember.

So when you see me limping by, you may notice that the bandages are gone and the splint has been removed. You may notice that the cane I once used is standing in the corner of my house by the front door. And as I walk down the street with the sun shining on my face, you may wonder, "How? How are you walking? How are you smiling? How are you enjoying today? How are you thankful? How are you praising? How are you still a family, filled with love for our Savior?

How?"

Well, friend, this is the reality
of being loved by our Savior,
knowing that the promise of this earthly life was that,
when everything else fell around us,
we would be held.

~ ~ ~

Appendix

"Held"

—Recorded by Natalie Grant
and written by Christa Wells

Two months is too little
They let him go
They had no sudden healing
To think that providence
Would take a child from his mother
While she prays, is appalling

Who told us we'd be rescued
What has changed and
Why should we be saved from nightmares
We're asking why this happens to us
Who have died to live, it's unfair

This is what it means to be held
How it feels, when the sacred is torn from your life
And you survive
This is what it is to be loved and to know
That the promise was when everything fell
We'd be held

This hand is bitterness
We want to taste it and
Let the hatred numb our sorrows
The wise hand opens slowly
To lilies of the valley and tomorrow

This is what it means to be held
How it feels, when the sacred is torn from your life
And you survive
This is what it is to be loved and to know
That the promise was when everything fell
We'd be held

If hope is born of suffering
If this is only the beginning
Can we not wait, for one hour
Watching for our Savior

This is what it means to be held
How it feels, when the sacred is torn from your life
And you survive
This is what it is to be loved and to know
That the promise was when everything fell
We'd be held

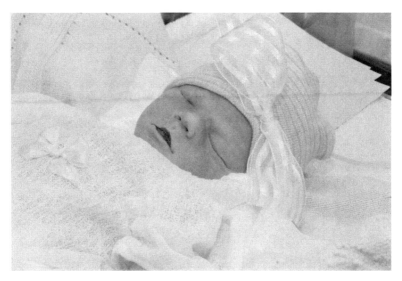

Piper Kay Brawner ~July 27, 2011 ~ 6lbs 12 oz., 20 inches

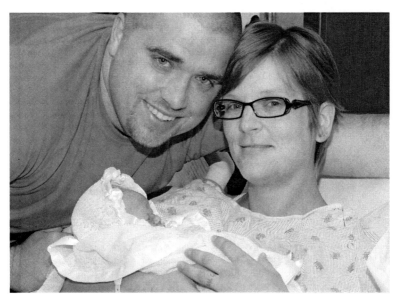

Although smiling through tears, we are
proud parents and Piper is our joy.

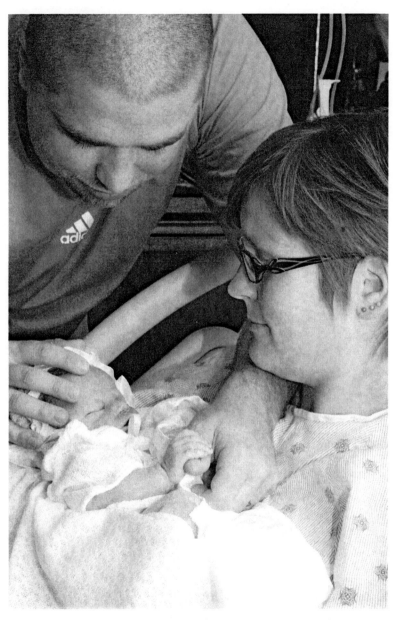

The moments of being able to touch Piper and
hold her will always be cherished.

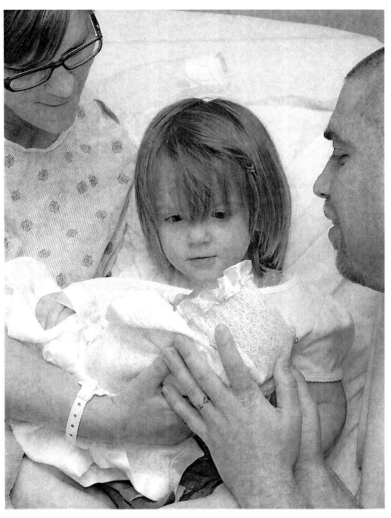

Adia is enthralled by her sister's beauty.

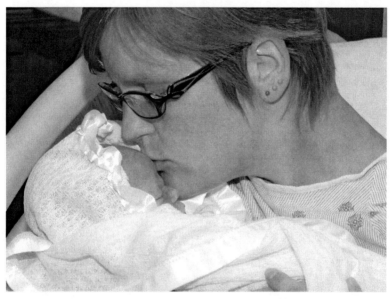

A mother's love...forever!

Adia spent time treasuring her sister's perfect features.

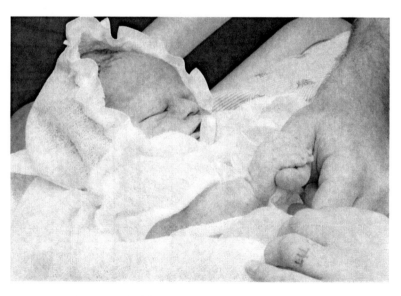

Piper is a daddy's girl! She looks just like him!

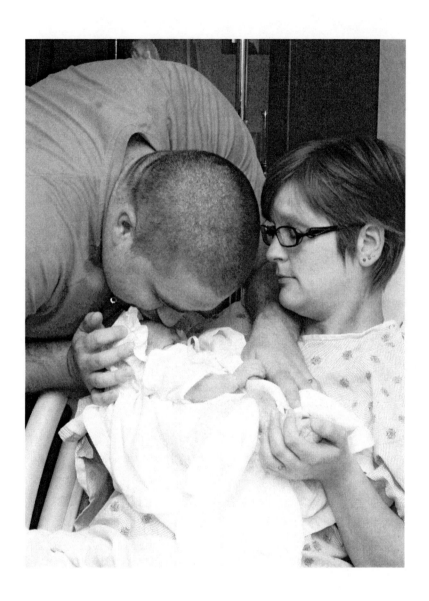

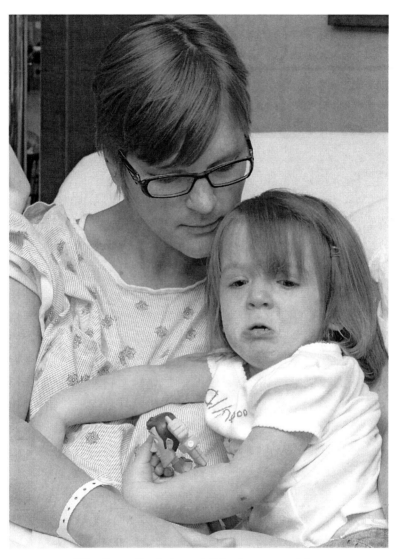

The face of pain in a child when something
she loves is torn from her arms.

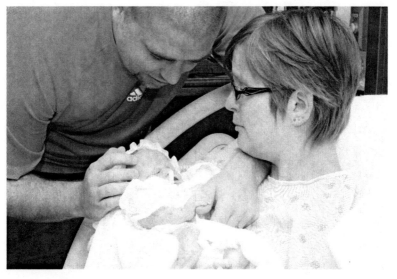

Pain mixed with sorrow as we say our goodbyes
and sing over Piper's sweet body.

Adia's joy upon releasing butterflies at her sister, Piper's funeral.

Her tiny but beautiful grave.
Hill Country Memorial Gardens Cemetery
New Braunfels, Texas.

Piper's tiny, white casket covered in beautiful
bright pink Gerber daisies.

In memory of Piper, the Artesian well, built through Holden
Uganda, will provide clean drinking water for many.

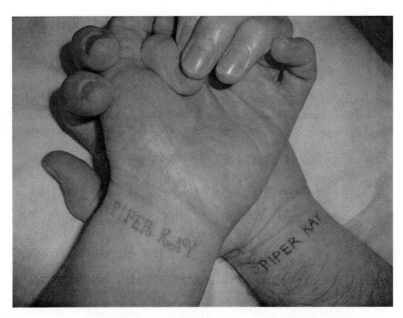

My pink and Dave's black tattoos constantly remind
us of our sweet Piper who is with Jesus.

Journals...

from the heart of one who has lost

"To all who mourn in Israel, he will give a crown of beauty
for ashes, a joyous blessing instead of mourning, festive praise
instead of despair. In their righteousness, they will be like great
oaks that the LORD has planted for his own glory."

Isaiah 61:3 (NLT)

[The email we sent to friends and family after our shocking news of losing Piper.]

July 29, 2011

These past few days have been filled with more emotion than was ever imaginable. We have learned that the Lord chooses to give and to take away, and our heart does choose to say, "Blessed be the name of the Lord."

We were able to love and cherish our Piper for nine months. She was born on Wednesday at 10:39 a.m., 6 lbs. 12 oz. and 20 inches long. She was beautiful, perfect, and peaceful. Just because we are not physically here with you now, we still cherish you all and wanted to thank you for your thoughts and prayers.

There will be a service on Monday, and we'd love it if you kept us in your thoughts and prayers. Thank you for your love.

In Christ ~ David, Julie & Adia Brawner

[Piper Kay Brawner's Obituary.]

"An Angel in the book of life wrote down my baby's birth.

And whispered as she closed the book "too beautiful for earth."

~Author Unknown.

Piper Kay Brawner ran to the arms of Jesus on Wednesday, July 27, 2011, at Ennis Regional Hospital in Ennis, TX. Although she was not on this earth for long, Piper touched the hearts and souls of many.

Piper is the beloved daughter of David and Julie Brawner and the beautiful sister of Adia Michele. She is greeted in heaven with open arms by Great Grandparents Charlie, Gladys, and Mary Brawner, Graham and Merle Cox, Irma Kruger, and Uncle David Brawner. Piper Kay is also cherished by her Great Grandparents Bud and Liz Looney of New Braunfels, Lawrence Kruger of Canada, Grandparents Steve and Sheila Cox of The Woodlands, Don and Karan Brawner of New Braunfels, Aunt Mollie Brawner of New Braunfels, Uncle Aaron and wife Kristi of The Woodlands and Uncle Brian Cox of The Woodlands and many other uncles, aunts, and cousins.

A graveside celebration will be held at the Hill Country Memorial Garden on Monday, August 1, 2011, at 10:00 am. We are asking that you share with us in wearing pink and white. In lieu of flowers, contributions may be made in Piper Kay's memory to the Piper Kay Brawner Memorial Scholarship at Deer Creek Camp, P.O. Box 200, Medina, TX 78055, or www.deercreekcamp. com where children can learn more about God's love.

"Surely, God is my salvation; I will trust and not be afraid. The Lord, the Lord, is my strength and my song; he has become my salvation," Isaiah 12:2.

Now I lay me down to sleep,
I pray the Lord my soul to keep,
If I shall die before I wake,
I pray the Lord my soul to take.
Amen

[The follow up email we sent to friends and family.]

August 7, 2011

These past few weeks have been a whirlwind of emotions. We wanted to take some time to sit down and say from the bottom of our hearts—thank you—and to share with you the God-breathed story of our Piper Kay.

I'm sure last week's email came to you with a shock—as did the news to us. Tuesday, the 26th, I went in for my normal check-up with the doctor. Dave wasn't with me because he was interviewing, and it was a normal check-up...we were thinking, "Let's ask her if we can induce! I'm due! We're so ready for Piper to be here!" They listened for the heartbeat and played it off like it was the machine not working. She did a quick ultrasound on me and calmly said she couldn't find all that she was looking for. She ordered another ultrasound to be done "STAT" at the hospital down the road. Within the hour, I was back in the doctor's office sitting on the bench...and I'll never forget the look on her face and tears in her eyes when she said that Piper Kay had gone to be with Jesus about two days prior. With tears streaming down my face, she said there is nothing I did or didn't do. That is was a mystery. There was no rhyme or reason. And as I sat there stunned in the doctor's office, telling myself to breathe in and out, she prayed with me.

Wednesday morning Dave and I went into the hospital to be induced. Piper was born at 10:39 am and was as beautiful as any baby has been. She was perfect. No cord wrapped. No problems with delivery. Nothing. She was perfect. The room was filled with a still peace as we held her and shared the few hours on earth together for the first and last time.

I share that with you because we have been richly blessed by you. I know that your thoughts and prayers have been with us.

We want you to know...God is present. Our hearts are, although overwhelmed with sorrow, filled with gratitude that as Aaron held up Moses' arms when he could no longer hold them up on his own, you are reaching out and holding our arms up. I promise you, we are not able to hold them up on our own. Thank you for your financial gifts, and know that we have started a fund in Piper's name at Deer Creek Sports Camp in Medina so that a child can go every summer in Piper's place and learn about our Jesus. You have helped make that happen for this coming summer.

The shock. The sudden realization of life versus death. The true understanding of the precious seconds to cherish. All within a moment our life has changed. We still have a family of four, but we have just lost and buried one. I cannot explain the depths of my soul that I have experienced. I did not know that there were such depths that existed, and yet when I cry...I cry from the depths. One thing I want you to know for certain is that I know we have been chosen for a reason. I know that the Lord our God knew that our sweet and precious Piper Kay would do more work for Him through her death that her life. That is hard for us to cough up, because we had such huge aspirations and hopes for our sweet baby girl. But Dave reminded me the other day of that truth. God is bigger. God is holding her. God is God. And as unfair as it may seem, we know beyond a shadow of a doubt that we will make it. We will be okay.

That peace that is beyond all of our understanding? Yeah, that peace? Dave and I want you to know that because you have walked with us, because you have been praying for us, we have had a glimpse into the depths of His peace that we never knew existed. Our souls that seemed to have opened so deeply have been overflowing with a peace that is unexplainable and a calmness that is beyond understanding. I am not in the least bit saying that the tears of sorrow do not flood into the void that cuts so deep. But in the midst of the tears burning down our face, in the midst of the inability to catch our breath when her sweet face is on our minds, His peace is so still and so consuming that we literally fall into His arms and sit with Him for a while.

Thank you for being there for us. You have touched our lives.

Much love from us to you. Dave, Julie and Adia

(By the way, a huge ministry and blessing to us was *Now I Lay Me Down to Sleep* photography that came and took photos for us. If you ever have anyone who experiences tragedy like ours, I would love for him or her to be blessed by the ministry and gift of pictures as we were. We were extremely hesitant, and a bit taken back by the thought, but would not trade them for the world now. Please share! www.nilmdts.org Adia sat with us in the hospital and with joy on her face, pointed to Piper. "Mommy, nose! Eyes! Mouth!" We told her, "Yes, sweet girl. That's your sister." We released butterflies for Piper, with our precious Adia helping. Thanks for being there in Spirit or in person. You are treasured.)

"*We Leave a Mark*" by Julie Brawner, published in *Texas Coach* and *TABC Newsletter*

I know that for most coaches, they are neck deep in football right now. Friday Night Lights flutter their heartbeat, and the anxiety that builds up to that 7:30 p.m. game is extremely intense. It's the beginning of the season. Everyone comes out the game to see this year's line of...coaches. It's true! Being the wife of a coach, I know that the first few games of any sport, parents and fans sit in the stands and—they size you up. Opinions are formed and some predict wins/losses individuals that, instead of sharing their negative votes, should focus more on getting their man-pony-tail trimmed up or looking for a shirt with sleeves attached. But, for what it's worth, they are the fans and...we need them. We need them in football, we need them in basketball, and we need them in baseball.

My husband and I had great plans for this season. As the Head Boy's Basketball Coach in Ferris, we had formulated plans and discussed our vision for this year. Little did we know, July 27 would change our lives and our plans forever. I was worried about how I would haul two little girls to games and support him, sitting with those fans in the stands that yell so loudly (me being one of them). But on July 27, we said goodbye to our full-term baby girl, Piper Kay. At the doctor's appointment the previous day, they could not find a heartbeat in my womb, and I delivered our precious baby girl on the 27. It was a shock. I was due the 30. He was ready for his post player to join the family. And instead of dribbling a ball, she was laid to rest in the beautiful Hill Country outside of New Braunfels. The Lord had numbered the days of our Piper Kay Brawner. Our two year old will not have a companion this season. But in full confidence and faith, we know that Piper will do more for His glory through her death than through her life on this earth. Still, without her here, this season will never be the same.

As we sit here, Friday Night Lights shining and the season fixing to be in full swing, other sports are getting ready too. It's a new school year full of potential. The football fields are lined and ready, the gym floors will be waxed, and the baseball fields will be watered and trimmed. As life has hit us with a huge curve ball, we realize that we have been seeing life through a fog that seems to be lifted. We are seeing a bit clearer now, that all these little things we stress about...all these wins and losses that we gauge our success upon? It is great. It feels good to win. But ultimately—is life about wins and losses? Is your season about statistical success? Looking at the face of death that day in the hospital, we realized that life is so fragile. Breath is not guaranteed. It is a gift. And the scale that we use as coaching families to gauge our success? We need to take a look at it and remember—it is about those kids out there. It is about molding them with good character, encouraging them to live a life of integrity, and teaching them to choose to step up and become men and women who will positively impact this world. It is about leading a life of example that those around can look and see that the men and women coaching their children will leave them better than when they found them.

We all leave our mark on life, in some form or fashion. I love being the wife of a coach. I wouldn't dream of my life any other way. This July, we were reminded that we are here for a reason. We are in this profession not just for those wins and losses. We are in it to leave an impact on this generation that surrounds us. As you look around at the boys or girls you come in contact with every day through their involvement in athletics, what mark are you leaving? What are you imprinting on the lives and hearts of these young men and women? What legacy will you leave behind? Because when it comes down to it—life is fragile. Handle it with care.

[My journals that I shared via email with close friends]

August 9, 2011

As I'm sitting in the recliner tonight, holding Adia so tight and rocking her with her music playing, I look around the room. I see her nightlight shining, the stars on the ceiling glowing, and the sign over the bed that I made for her when she was in my belly those 2 ½ years ago. *Adia Michele* and below it states *God's gift; like God.* Tears begin streaming down my face as I pray for my two girls. As her name states, Adia is God's gift. She is His gift to us and so many, and He knew that we would endure such hardships in life...and boy did He know we would need a precious gift like her. My prayer for her has always been that her life would be one that is a blessing to all she comes in contact with and that she would be a gift to every person she touches. Now, more than ever before, I see God at work in her precious life. And as I prayed for her, I remembered the funeral...and how her precious face lit up everyone's heart. She is a true gift, and I pray that she would continue to become more and more "like God".

Oh, and our sweet Piper.

As the tears streamed down my face, I ask God to hold her close and tell her that the three of us...we miss her terribly. And to tell her that we love her very much. But I thank God over and over for His faithfulness in keeping my precious baby girl from any pain, any suffering, any sin. Warm tears rolled down my cheeks, down my neck, and I was blessed. *Piper Kay* means *Joyous spirit; happy, rejoicing.* It hit me today. Our Piper Kay. Our sweet child. She will know nothing other than the purity of a joyous spirit. She will sing nothing but songs of rejoicing. She will experience nothing but the true essence of happiness. Wow! God knew.

He knew when we named Adia; she was His gift to us. He knew when we named Piper; her spirit would be filled with the purest joyfulness. She is in the best place possible. She is with our Savior.

I know that these are ramblings that come from a heart of confusion. I know that when I sit and rock Adia, I think of crazy things that I want to share with someone. And as I sat there tonight, I realized I wanted to share them with you. I have to say that I am full to the brim with an overwhelming reminder of the precious family I have…you. I consider you family, though not through human blood, rather Christ's. You are near and dear to my existence…now, more than ever before. And trust me, I don't say that to just anyone. You know me better than that!

So expect more rambling from me…sent directly to you. And feel free to forward on these words if you *ever* think they may encourage someone else. Like I said, I literally sit in the quietness of the night and think. And then, attempt to regurgitate it on paper…because I have to share it. I'm a sharer at heart. Good night, sweet brothers and sisters. You have blessed my life.

August 10, 2011

Wounds. I thought I had begun to bandage them up. I thought I had already put on the splint, wrapped up my sores, casted the break. Little did I know that at any moment, the salt from the tears that poured from the depths of my soul could rip open those bandages and remind me of the freshness of the pain I just endured.

She's never coming back. As I sat in the room with the door closed, I looked over pictures placed in a collage frame with "FAMILY" engraved in the center. Ten pictures. As I scanned over those pictures, attempting to place them in the best spot, tears began to gush. She's never coming back.

Gorgeous. Beautiful. All ten fingers and all ten toes. Her nose is like her daddy's. Her eyes are like her daddy's. Does she look like me at all? Smile. Death. Tears. Precious. Pain...oh, so much pain. As thoughts are pouring through my head and down through my eyes and nose, I'm overwhelmed by how much this hurts and how it is something out of my control and that I can never fix it. There is a picture of me holding her feet, and as my husband walked in the room and tears began rolling down his face, my hand went towards the picture of her sweet feet, and I grazed it with my thumb. Never again will I feel those feet. Never again will I hold them and feel the softness of her precious skin. Never. For in Heaven, she'll have a new body.

My soul is aching, and although I trust that God is holding me, I'm broken. My pieces are shattered. My soul is overwhelmed. I know that my precious Adia Michele is lying in the room next to me and sleeping soundly, but I yearn for her to know her sister. My husband and I long for Adia and Piper to play, laugh, jump, dance, and sing together. I don't want to wait until Heaven! I know that Piper is in the arms of my Savior, but that will never negate the pain of the piercing in our souls. She was fully formed. She was full-term. She was ready to enter the world. She was beautiful. She was taken. She is gone.

The bandages unraveled today. Who knew that at any given moment, this broken human being could drop the jar in which all my pieces had been gathered. Walking takes huge amounts of efforts. I've had to remind myself to breath in and out. I've had to gasp for air when the crying came from so deep within my soul. I've had to remind myself to shampoo my hair, to get out of the shower, to put one foot in front of the other and keep walking. And yet, as I look at myself in the mirror and am reminded that my body tells me I've just had a baby, I realize that as much as this hurts…I am okay that it happened to me. I would take this yoke from anyone, if I could.

As I head to bed with a massive headache from crying all my tears, the image of my sweet baby's feet are engrained in my head and I will continue to yearn for her touch. I will continue to ache for her kiss. And I will dream sweet painful dreams of tucking her hair behind her ear and telling her, "Pipe…you're sweet. I love you."

August 11, 2011

Tonight is the first night we've been alone. Since our news of the loss of Piper, family and friends have surrounded us. What an amazing blessing it has been. I've had people to cry with, people to make me laugh, people to lay with me while I put my head in a blanket and wept like I've never wept before. And now, we are alone. Not excited about it.

Anxiety has swept in, and I've been battling it off for the past few days. Going back to work. Well, I thought I'd be tapping into the FMLA and holding a baby girl right now, taking my 6-12 weeks and cuddling a newborn. How quickly life changes. So now, the decision comes…going back to work? I knew it would be stressful, going back with two little ones. Now one is in Heaven being well taken care of, and the other is in an in-home pre-k… also being well taken care of. Then, there is me. Mrs. Brawner—a fifth grade math teacher. High stress. How do I go back? How do I face classrooms full of kids? How do I tell children that I taught last year that Piper never made it into this world alive? How do I overcome the exhaustion that engulfs me? How?

I know that if I do not take care of myself this year, we are all going to crumble. If I hit work head-on, with our commute and dropping off/picking up Adia, our days get very short, and it is the same routine. That routine does not leave much room for sweet family time. After a loss like Piper Kay, it is amazing how perspective changes, and the realizations of life become very clear on some things. I'm not willing to sacrifice time with my precious Adia and my phenomenal husband. Not going to do it! Stress is not worth it. Busyness is not something to be proud of! Life needs to be slowed down in the Brawner household...and every minute, every breath needs to be treasured.

All that to say, life is fuzzy again. In the mass chaos of what has sideswiped our family, I feel confused and lost as to what we are to do. I know that God has asked us to endure this tragedy for a reason, and my heart's desire is to honor Him in everything. But where does Julie need to be this year to heal? I know there will be scars, but if I don't treat the wound and care for it, infection will set in, and I'm not willing to risk my healing process. Lord, what do I do? Where do I go?

If you say, "Go", we will go. If you say, "Stay", we will stay. If you say, "Step out on the water"...and they say it can't be done... we'll fix our eyes on you and we will come.

August 14, 2011

Church. A great place to be, a tough place to enter. As we headed back to our church on Sunday, I was excited for Adia to play and to be in His house. Tears overwhelmed me as we entered and began the service. Songs of love, grace, His goodness...all so true. Words could not make it out of my mouth, so I stood there with my lungs barely open and tears streaming down my cheeks, making puddles on my shirt. Words could not be formulated, but unlike ever before, I felt the Spirit of the Most High God interceding on my behalf. I was singing, though not in my petty voice, but what seemed like the voice of angels, and from the depths of my soul. Yes, our God is good. Yes, our God is full of love. And yes, I will go where you send me.

It makes no sense. Why take my child? Why all the pain and anguish? Why is Piper with you right now and not cradled in my arms and nuzzled up against me? It's for your glory. It's not about me. It's just not. How selfish to sit and wish for her to endure the pains of this life, just so I can hold her. How selfish of me to wish breath in this sinful world when all she knows is the breath of Christ. Oh, she was saved for a special place in Heaven. She is cradled against the chest of Christ, and that is much warmer than mine.

Church? Well, the people in the row in front of us were probably wondering why on earth these crazies behind them were weeping and gasping for air. They were probably wondering why our salty tears were splotching their blonde summer hair and dripping on their iPhones as they checked their Facebook status. But I didn't care. We didn't care. We sat there, in a pool of salty tears, not understanding this tremendous loss…but knowing with complete confidence that our God is good.

August 15, 2011

Most of my thoughts seem to hit in the quietness of rocking Adia, or in the fuzziness that I now know are my attempt at brain waves in my state of being. We went to the mall the other day and walked around. "Why is it that she gets to keep her baby and I didn't?" Wow, the thoughts that pop into my head at any given moment. And I hear the whisper of God, "Piper is special, Julie. I will accomplish so much through her life! Just trust me."

Her life. Nine months. I sat there tonight and rocked my breathing child. I couldn't help but begin to cry as she grabbed my left arm and placed it on her back. She grabbed my right arm and wrapped it around the other side of her. My chest began heaving, and I cried out a few audible wails with my arms wrapped tightly around Adia. And my sweet child, my two-year-old baby girl, began to mimic her mother. She began a few faint cries, just like mine. She knew I was hurting. I thought back to when I was rocking Adia three weeks ago, Piper in my belly kicking her sister and saying through her kicks, "You're sitting on me, Adia!" Nine months. Oh, how I wish I had cherished those months more. Oh, how I crave to have that time back again…to sing to her every night, to rub her feet, her arms, her body through my belly, and to tell her every day how much I love her. Oh, how I yearn to have that time back and instead of hating every moment of being pregnant and fat—to treasure it. Dave and I have talked about that often. Nine months. Thank you, Lord, for those nine months.

I began singing Adia a song out of the back of her Little Golden Book, *Prayers for Children*. We have always sung a revamped version to her. "Now we lay Adia down to sleep. We pray thee Lord, thy child to keep. Thy love guard her through the night, and wake her with the morning light." I'm sure the words are wrong. And I am most positive that the tune her father and I sing it in is most incorrect. But, it's the Brawner-version of our special song. We've always sung it to her before bed. Until Piper.

It's been hard to sing to Adia at night since we lost Piper. Why? Because as Dave held Piper Kay Brawner, all 6 lbs. 12 oz. of her, there came the moment when we had to say goodbye. And as we touched the head of our baby girl, we did not say goodbye. Instead, we sang to her…and we sang just that. "Now we lay Piper down to sleep. We pray thee Lord, our child to keep.

Thy love guard her through the night, and wake her with the morning light."

So, as I sang that to Adia tonight, my chest began to pant up and down and my breath became harder and harder to grasp. She is gone. And I whispered to Adia, "We sang this to your sister, Piper." She curled up next to me as close as she could, tucked her arms in, and in tears I claimed Christ, His blood, and His protection over us. "I love you, Adia. I love you." In Piper's nine months here with us—God is going to do a lifetime of change. She knows the embrace of God. She knows His touch. My prayer? My hope? My hearts ache? That God will be fair and just, and hold my precious Adia Michele just as close as He holds her sister...and that through Adia's life; He uses her to impact every person she comes in contact with.

Oh, how death gives you such a huge glimpse into the hugeness of life. God had to look into the face of His son and watch as death overtook His body on earth. On a much smaller scale, I've had to look into the face of my child and experience the same. What a reminder that every second of every day matters. Death is real. But...praise Him; it is not to be feared. For someday, we will experience death—and what joy to be caught up with Him and on the horizons, see Piper's dancing feet and upward arms welcoming me home with her.

August 19, 2011

I was asked today if I was a reflective writer. I'm not sure what that means in its fullest sense, but I had to sit back and say, "Yes, I surely think that I am." Writing helps me to process what, right now, are unchartered waters for me. It helps me collect the mass of thoughts that swarm my head. It helps me to digest the chaos of daily life. It is needed. And I hadn't written? I'd be lost.

This week has been...overwhelming. I think that may be the word. Currently, I have a massive migraine beginning behind my right eye down the back of my neck and into my arm. It's been a day, to say the least. I went back to work. And, although some may think that the teaching profession is one that is stress-less, I would have to disagree. It has been full of stress—plenty to go around!

On Saturday I was panicked and engulfed by the anxiety of entering back into the work world. Could I do it? Would I succeed? Would it be okay? Will I crumble? And nobody could tell me what I should or should not do. So, I tried.

In-service. As I sat there Monday morning, the first day in weeks that I've attempted to put on makeup, listening to the Superintendent go over TAKS results, my brain began to get "fuzzy". This is something I have never encountered before. I have never felt this fuzzy feeling that takes over and makes everything hazy. It was as if I was on the Charlie Brown show hearing, "Wa wa wa wa wa wa wa wa." I tried to pay attention, but could not function correctly. I tried to follow directions, but could not remember what anyone had just said. Wow. Had I taken a dose of that sleeping medication they gave me?? No. This was reality.

As the week progressed, I dove into work and it was...okay. The support of co-workers has been phenomenal. But as tough as I am and as hard as I tried, I am making the decision to take my leave of absence. I can say that I tried my best. I can promise that I did everything in my ability to perform at work. And I can say, now, that I have complete confidence that I do not need to be in a classroom on Monday morning. Wow.

My word to describe this week? Burden. I have been shouldering a burden that felt like it weighed 1000 pounds. Every day was a choice to get up, take a step, put on clothes, and wake up my precious baby girl in the next room for school. Every day was full of every ounce of effort I had—to speak without tears, to talk without confusion, and to exist without a look of emptiness. And I tried. I had to take a step back and say, "It's not worth it." It is not worth it to our family to push me into work with *hopes* that I would succeed. It is vital to the healing of these wounds that I take some time to reflect...to write...to process. If I do not, I will not survive.

Death. When I walk in a room, I bring death with me. Others are constantly watching and observing. The ability to survive through such a trauma astonishes people. The mere fact that I can drive, talk, walk, and breathe in and out is shocking to most individuals. And yet why do they not ask me how I am? Why am I in the midst of hundreds of people, and yet I feel so alone? Death.

I have come to realize that everyone in this life has no idea how to handle this situation. What do you do when someone's baby dies? What do you say to her? How do you handle her? And I've had to take a step back and tell myself, "I don't know what to do, say, or think about myself...much less expect others around me to know what to say to me!" What an eye-opener! What a learning experience. Piper has not been gone for long, and it is an extremely odd situation. Yet I yearn for people to ask me about her. I desire to share my story, if people will hear it. I would love for someone to touch my shoulder, to hug me, to pat me on the back. No words are necessary. They are most definitely welcomed, but even a shoulder squeeze that says, "I'm thinking about you!" would be most encouraging. And yet as much as I crave that, I step back and understand...they don't know. They care. They hurt right along with me. They tear up at the thought of my precious Piper Kay. They question the "Why?" and yearn for answers.

They are standing with me, attempting to stay afloat—but they are with me.

Oh, my soul yearns for hugs sometimes. It cries out for discussion. My eyes long to pour tears. My heart desires to break. I can see the pain in the eyes of those around me as they look at me...and I know—they love me.

August 20, 2011

Fair. What a word. You can't really sit there and reflect on that word because—guess what? Life is not fair. Today has been an interesting day. A morning filled with chatting with a friend, and an afternoon of my body entering into a zombie-like state. I made it through the day, but my thoughts were absent. I was extremely aware of the fact that I had to tell myself to move my feet to walk and pick up my arm to get the fork to my mouth.

I pulled out the lawn chair tonight as Dave was putting Adia to sleep. I turned off all the lights outside and sat in the driveway. As I looked up at the vastness of space and yearned to see through the clouds to Heaven, the warmth of tears began to cover my cheeks. It is amazing how—after you've been through something like this—it does not matter when you cry, how you cry, or if your mascara runs all over your face. Crying becomes part of life, and everyone else can just deal with my mascara smudges!

I sat out there in complete darkness. It was just me and God...and Pipe's little solar bush that we bought that matches the one on her grave. Its pink flowers were glowing beside me. "I miss her, Lord! I miss her!" I pulled out my phone and gazed at the pictures I had of our family with her. What color were her eyes? What would her voice have sounded like? I knew she was active, because she sure did kick a lot! What sports would she have played? Why can I not have her here with me?

I ask these questions and deep down, I know. I know that God chose her, and He knew that through her death, lives would be changed here on earth. Not just lives, but TONS of lives…and people will come to know Jesus because of her. But I sat there in tears and told God that it is not fair. It is not fair that she beat us. I am overwhelmed with gratitude that Piper has never known pain. She has never cried a tear or skinned a knee. She has only known the arms of Jesus and the warmth of Heaven's glow. I looked up to the sky and told God, "It's not fair. It is not fair that Piper gets to be with you and Adia does not. It's not fair that we cannot give Adia what you can give Piper! That Adia has to scrape her knees and know what tears are and go through the pain of life here on earth. And so…Lord, you better use Adia and change the world with her. Because I can't give her the life that you've granted Piper, but I yearn for her to experience your warmth, touch, and glow just as her sister knows."

I love my baby girls. I want the best for them. And I am comforted to know that my Piper Kay is beaming in the glow of Heaven. I miss her terribly. I want her near. But I know she is taken care of, better than I ever could. I wish she could cry on my shoulder, I wish she would wake me up at all hours of the night…but that is so selfish of me. Life is not fair. It's life.

August 24, 2011

People ask if I feel as if a burden has been taken off my shoulders—considering the decision to take my leave of absence. My answer? Yes. But I feel as if another burden has been given…the burden of a scarlet letter. As I work down my "to do" list of all the things that I thought I'd never get done and now have a chance to tackle,

I realize that I'm entering the real world. I am entering into the world where no one knows what has happened to our family just a few short weeks ago. As I walk in and out of stores, run errands, and buy groceries…no one knows my secret. Can I have a scarlet letter please?

Although strangers have no clue about our current trials, I feel like I want to share. I know that it is most uncomfortable for people to accept the news of our tragedy. Dave and I were discussing that we feel like wherever we go, whether we join a small group at church or simply attempt to meet new people, we come with huge baggage and drop a bomb on any and every situation. We are the epitome of drama, at the current moment. And so for that sake, I wish I could wear a pin with Piper's picture on it or stamp something across my forehead. Maybe I could make a bumper sticker or t-shirt so people knew I was coming.

I went to meet with my doctor on Monday about taking time off. Same deal. I walk in and they know me by name. The office is silent—"You can take a seat Mrs. Brawner." When I get called back, I can tell that the entire office is hurting with me. The nurse chats with me as tears fill her eyes. The doctor hugs me with compassion and supports me 110 percent. With my presence comes the sight of death. And I would venture to say that the majority of those living are terrified of death. So, they make the decision to simply not approach death…or me. But you know what? Once you have looked death in the face and realized that our days are truly numbered—what God said in His Book is TRUE—death is no longer feared. That is what the disciples knew! They looked at death in the face of their Christ, and they realized…this life is not where it ends! This life is a mere speck in the vastness of eternity! I know that when people look at me or hear me say I've lost my child, they run. But please—do not flee! I know you have questions that are instantaneously filling your mind. I know you wonder about the hows, whys, ifs, buts…and I know you may be speechless. But stay. Sit with me a while. And learn that death is not to be feared.

You're probably thinking by know, this chick is ca-razy! And I often think that of myself too. How can I sit here and say God is "good"—but I'm not holding my baby girl? How can I sit here and say God knows "best"—but Piper is not here in our loving family? Well…I feel like we view life now from a completely different vantage point. I have often felt like I'm watching everyone else's life go by, and they're in this glass box. They hurt, yes. They are hustling and bustling, singing praises to God and loving one another. And then there's Dave and me…on the outside looking in. We hurt, but to depths that we cannot even use words to explain. We cry, but with tears that are so moist and warm that they are unfamiliar. We hurt every moment of every day without ceasing. We attempt to sing, but the words cannot squeak out of our mouths. We love, but with a deeper love than we have ever imagined, known, experienced, or touched before. We have faith, but not the faith that we've had in times past. This faith is far from a feeling. It is based upon complete trust, honest acknowledgement that God is God, and truth that does not and will not question His holiness. We have felt the touch of God, the peace that truly is beyond our understanding, and we are speechless. We have looked at death—in the face of our child—and have acknowledged God to be God. We have chosen to trust that He is whom He promises to be and that He had Piper's precious days numbered. And by *His grace*, I can honestly sit here and say that I believe Him to be true, I believe Him at His word, and I know in the depths of my being that He knew she would pass away. He knew she would spend nine months here…and He knew the exact time, day, and moment that He would cradle Piper Kay Brawner in His arms as He sang songs over her. He knew. He wanted her. He is God. I am not. And I trust Him…as my Savior, as my Lord, and as my precious loving Father. Crazy? Yes. But isn't that faith?

August 25, 2011

I tried a new Bible Study group last night. Yes, a round of applause would be appreciated. I have never felt so nervous to go and sit with women I didn't know. I have never felt so alone, like a target. Will it be okay? Do I drop this bomb of death on them tonight? Will they support me—or flee from me? Just go in, sit down, and introduce yourself. The awkward words squeaked out of my unconfident self, "My name is Julie Brawner."

You see, we are out here in the middle of a town and place we are unfamiliar with. Dave took a head boys' basketball coaching job to work for a man that we fell in love with, Coach Randy Barnes. We knew no one. We knew nothing about the stores or the area or the communities. We moved, cold turkey, to the town of Waxahachie, Texas, so we could coach and love on kids in Ferris. We had no idea that we would face this trial, so fresh and so new, so alone, and so far from the friends and family we love so dearly.

What is encouraging to know is that God has ordained every day of our lives, every moment of our existence. He knows what we need. He knows when we need it. He has a plan, and it is written out. Our mighty God has taken the time to count every hair on our head and know every thought in our foggy minds. I know that. And with every particle of my being, I believe it—I'm taking Him at His Word. He used my precious husband to encourage me to go to this Coach's Wives' Bible Study…and God knew, an eternity in advance, that open arms would embrace me. Women who had never met me, seen me, and known my name—they were ready to hear about Piper Kay, and they were gentle and compassionate enough to embrace me and beg me to be a part. It is not like that in every small group. God knew—He's said it! His Words are truth. Why don't we really believe them? This life alter has been an amazing test to see if Dave and I will take our God at His Word. You better believe, I'm holding fast to every one—and I'm holding Him to His promises. He is faithful, and I know He will follow through.

I've done a lot of thinking today. It has been difficult being home alone, allowing myself to take the time to think about Piper and to grieve. I'm taking a leave of absence and yet—there is no baby at home for me to care for. Weird. I hate being sad. It's not fun. As I look in the mirror every morning, I see this maternity stricken body and cringe. Eww! 166.5 lbs. still? Because I don't have an infant in the next room, it is hard to remember that this body just endured the birthing of a child. Surely that is not how God had intended us, pre-sin, to labor and give birth! Surely not! Although the time in the hospital always seems to be foggy, I do recall the tremendous pain of contractions, the inability to get an epidural in time, and the painful birthing of a child! Oh…man! Did that really just happen to my body? It did. So I decided to lay down for a bit, something I have not done in…who knows how long! At 2 p.m., when I finally saw through the cloudiness of my sleepy eyes, I realized I had just slept 5 hours. Oops!

Time off from work may leave me stir-crazy. There will be days where I feel embarrassed, guilty even, that I am staying home and have no Piper to care for. But I am realizing that my body needs to rest and recover. If I do not, I will not exist. I cannot thank God enough for the gift of Adia Michele during this time in our lives. I get to wake up to her groggy "I hate the morning" face and play with Pooh Bear and the honey pot that she loves so dearly. I am blessed to watch her run (like a girl!) and dance to music. And when her little eyes look up at me as she rocks her

Tinkerbell and says, "Baby!"…I quickly realize how much I hurt for her and wish, so badly, she had her baby sister here with her. I look in Adia's face and get glimpses of Piper. She smiles, and I see Piper. They look so much alike. It is hard to tell one baby picture from the other. I've realized, again, in the quietness of this week, that Piper is never coming home. She will never be in another family picture; she will never take a bath with her big sister; she will never meet a man and fall in love; and her daddy will never walk her down the isle. Oh—my heart hurts so badly, just thinking about these truths.

For the rest of this life, Adia will always remind me of her sister. There will be moments to come that, as Adia passes the ball in her first basketball game, I'll realize that I'll never see Piper do that. I do not know what will come in our future. But what I do know is that I have a precious, living daughter who is a gift to us. We are entrusted with her here on earth, and her days are numbered as well. So, we are challenged to take every moment, cherish every laugh, love and kiss and hug her—because who knows how long we have together? Life is too short to forget what is important. Seize the moment. For real.

August 26, 2011

I looked down at my phone after I dropped Adia off today, and my heart stopped. It felt like it had skipped a beat, literally. It felt hard in my chest, my breathing stopped, my stomach got hard…and my lips began to quiver. I've never dreaded a day so much—tomorrow is the 27.

I began bawling. Tears have come many times a day, but the gut wrenching sobs? Not often. I try to contain those. But on the way home, I wondered how many people could see through my windows as my body shook from the sobs. My face turned red, and my head began to pound from the tears. I replayed over and over today—one month ago. Ready, waiting for Piper...went to do laundry that day. And then the doctor's appointment: July 26, 2:00 p.m. Funny how those things will stick to my brain forever. No heartbeat. No heartbeat. No heartbeat.

I literally feel like mine has stopped for the moment. I want to know my baby. I feel like I do. I feel like I know what she would have been like, the things she would have loved, the sports she would have played...from nine months in the womb, I truly feel like I knew my baby girl. I know a lifetime for us is a spec in the midst of eternity. But today, it feels like my lifetime will be an eternity—because I have to wait that long until I can brush her hair, dance with her, twirl her around, and tell her that I love her.

Why is it that some, instead of doctor's visits, have monthly cemetery visits? One month—she should be—tomorrow. And instead of a healthy check-up, instead of a celebration, there is me...sitting in a pool of tears, wondering how we find joy in the midst of this intense sorrow.

Lord, you promise to intervene on our behalf. I need you, dear Jesus, to be my intercessor today and tomorrow...because I need, crave, yearn to find joy in the midst of this sorrow. Help me. Help Dave. We cannot make it alone. We need your touch more than ever before.

August 27, 2011

Ouch. Just looking at the date makes me realize it has been a month. I think that from now on, every "27" will be a reminder of Piper. The tattoo on my wrist, "Piper Kay", will be a reminder. Celebrating birthdays will be a reminder. And that...is okay.

I never want to forget. I never want to leave Piper Kay out of the Brawner family. She is and will forevermore be a Brawner. The memories of her, although they are moments, will remain for a lifetime. And we will carry her beyond nine months. We will carry her through this journey of life—and will walk with her for eternity.

It has been two days of complete contemplation. I do not like God's plan for us right now, in this moment. I do not feel good about the fact that I cannot cuddle Piper and wake up with her in the night. I miss her so very much, and this pain has left us—crippled. I realized this is the perfect way to explain our state-of-being. This tragedy will leave a mark on Dave and I forever. It is not something that will go away—it is not an experience that "in time" will fade. We lost our child. We buried our baby girl. She did not breath; she did not have life here on earth; she is not coming back. That will leave you crippled. But—and I'm laughing at the sweet thoughts—did Jesus not heal the crippled? Did he not extend his hand and say, "Pick up your mat and walk!"? Wow! He will not leave us here. He will heal us. It will leave scars, maybe even a limp. But I will limp my way through the remainder of this life here on earth because I know, at the end of this race, is the face of my Christ—and He will be holding the hand of my daughter, and in unison they will shout, "Welcome home!"

A rollercoaster of emotions has hit in these past two days. We are too far from the grave to visit it and make sure it is beautiful, because she deserves nothing less. So Dave's precious family has ensured that on this day, they would visit—knowing and acknowledging that it has been one month. This month has dragged by. Moment by moment we have existed through it. And yet in the same breath, we can say it has flown by. One month already? She would have been one month. As I looked at the picture of her grave on my phone, immediately my rollercoaster hit that turn and dropped its 50-foot drop. My heart was in my stomach. My breath was non-existent.

"Piper Kay Brawner—July 27, 2011." Just the sight of the headstone was enough to shoot me over the edge. You can't run from the truth when it is imprinted permanently on a sign. Our baby girl. Our Piper Kay. Her tiny little 6 lb. 12 oz. body is laid to rest in the ground right below. Although I hate this moment, although I've dreaded this day...I can say in complete confidence that our God will not leave us crippled. Our God will command us to get up and walk. And as we do, lives will be changed. God will do His miraculous work, and through the life and death of Piper, we will experience the tender touch of our Savior. I must say, though it is difficult, it is amazing to be part of such a huge plan.

Already, God is doing His work through our baby girl. It hurts. We yearn for her touch. We desire her presence in this household. We wish she were in her crib listening to lullaby's right now. But she is not...and as I lay my head to rest tonight, I will remember those last few moments on earth that we held. I will remember her daddy leaning over, kissing her forehead as I wept...and saying "We love you Piper Kay Brawner. We love you."

August 30, 2011

I know as time goes on, days will begin to get easier. The thought of Piper will never go away, but the pain will begin to not pierce so deep, and the memories will become sweeter and sweeter. It has been like that today. The Lord has placed His hedge around us, and I feel comforted. Even though a glimpse at the grave of my baby girl brings immediate tears, the pictures of her overwhelm me with pride—I'm a proud mother of two.

I can sit and talk for hours about my baby girls...and both of their stories. Sometimes I lose my words and get choked up. Sometimes I get so excited I'm talking a million miles an hour. Either way, I've got stories to share about both of them—but what I have learned is that people are terrified to ask. Don't get me wrong, I have many that have rallied around me and do ask me all the time how I am doing. But it is amazing how people flee from the sight of death. They run from the pain that comes with loss. They become mute at the topic of tragedy. Oh dear friends...do you not realize? When you flee from us, you may dodge the pain for a while, but you miss out on the huge blessings and joyous tears of the sweet memories?

I've spoken with so many people that have endured loss and death. Not just death of a child, but of a husband or father or mother. Death. It is something that is viewed as ugly, awful, hush-hush. It hurts. No matter what the loss, it is something sacred that has been torn from your life. I am overwhelmed by the fact that they share this plague with me. They are marked by death as well—and they have experienced the feeling of others lacing up their tennis shoes and running as far and fast as they can in the other direction. Funny thing is, are we not all marked by death? Why is it so feared? Why are *we* so feared?

I understand what some may think. I understand how some may feel. "I just don't know what to say" or "I don't want to mess up or hurt them more." I'll tell you one thing that I have learned from my loss. I will never again be afraid of my words. I will never again be afraid of giving a hug or squeezing a shoulder. I may stutter over my words or tear up or bawl on their shoulder with them, but I will seize every opportunity to touch the life of someone who has experienced loss—of *any* kind. Because I'll tell you one thing, this family who is marked by death? The Brawners? We want to brag about our baby girl, and we would take a hug or pat on the back any day. It does not have to be words. It does not have to be touch. A note. A card. A smile. That is what people surviving a loss crave. They crave people to acknowledge their loss, to look in their direction with kindness and not horror, and say, "Sweet one, I hurt *with* you." I am the voice of those around you whose eyes are downcast, whose tears flow at every church service, or whose walk is lonely. Just a touch means the world and will never be forgotten.

August 31, 2011

I had my six weeks post-partum appointment today. I had been thinking a lot about Piper today. It is amazing how proud I can be of a child that never walked this earth with me. But I am. Walking into the doctor's office, you could sense the complete compassion that oozed from every one of their souls. Piper has left her mark. God has used her to share the story of hope with the world—that in the face of death, there is the light of hope that shines so brightly, none can resist.

The check-up went fine, just like the previous nine months had gone. I am healthy. I am good. And there is no reason to think that I cannot have children again. I felt like I flooded her with questions. Was there anything at all wrong with me, the pregnancy, the delivery, and the placenta? No, all was perfect. Does this increase my chance in having another stillbirth? No, this just...happened. Can I have children again? Yes, physically you could get pregnant in a month or so. But emotionally—only time will tell. Does this put me as a high-risk patient the next time I get pregnant? With any good doctor, yes it would.

It is a mystery. All ask "Why?" and I know why. Because Piper Kay Brawner will impact this world through her death in ways that would have been impossible through her life. Is that fair? Not in our terms. Does it hurt? Goodness, yes! But does God have a

131

plan? Absolutely. And it is one to prosper us and not to harm us. It is one of hope and a future. Piper only knows the pure love of her Heavenly Father. She is safe in His arms. Does it seem right that this happened to our family? That He took our baby girl away? No. But we live in a broken, fallen, messed-up world that needs to see the light of our Savior. And through our family, through our Piper, her joyous spirit will light the way for many.

Adia and Piper would have had so much fun dancing together. They would have giggled and jumped, spun and twirled. As I look at my living daughter tonight, her big blue eyes astound me. What a gift. God has given me Adia Michele, and she is my gift. As her little bob haircut waves in the wind, I smile with pride. My oldest daughter…my spice ball. She would have made the world's best older sister (in my opinion!). I can only hope that someday she will have that opportunity. But just as Piper will do huge things through her life, I am confident that our Adia will live her life for Jesus Christ. I believe to my depths that she will continue to become more and more like God…and I trust God to use her and touch the lives of every person she comes in contact with. I pray that over her, almost every night. So someday, when she is reading this, she will know—"I have big plans for you, baby girl… but our God has even greater plans. Hold on tight, never let go, and your daddy and I will smile as we watch you soar. For now, sweet child, I love you. I treasure you…good night."

On a more frustrated note, I must say that as I see the white tips of her ugly two-year molars attempting to break through, I wonder if tonight will be a night of sleep or sleeplessness. As I hear her cry and scream in the middle of the night I know, sleep is out of the question. I lay with her and she snuggles up to me. Her little body tosses and turns and she is constantly saying, "No…no…" but her eyes aren't open. She wants to touch me and know that I am there. I begin to pray that the Lord would make these teeth

BREAK THROUGH! I'm tired of them! We've been getting no sleep for...a month now, or more. Especially adding molars on top of what we deal with moment-by-moment! So I pray, "Lord, calm her down. Put your hand on her and rock her to sleep—she needs it." Adia rolls and fidgets and tosses and turns. All she says is, "No...no." At this point, I begin to get angry. My mind starts growling and thinking that with Piper, I'm not sitting here asking "Why?" I trust my God to be greater than my thoughts and my ways. I trust Him at His words. But come on—can I get a break here? Will you heal my breathing baby and grant her sleep? Will you help her teeth break through? In the grand scheme of things, these are dinky little requests compared to the junk we've just dealt with, so...GOD, you need to answer them!!!!!!

And in my frustrated prayers, I hear again that quiet whisper, "Julie, I've got her—and you. I hear you. Trust me." I laugh, His peace releases the tension in my body, and I sink into the bed more comfortably. You know, I trust that He is answering. Maybe Adia is having bad dreams and needs me laying here with her, cuddling and snuggling and telling her that I love her. Or maybe, just maybe, God knew that tonight was a night that my soul needed to be snuggled with—and he sent her, my precious Adia Michele. Oh God, you take care of me. You hold me. You provide. Thank you for being...good. I believe—help me in times of unbelief.

September 2, 2011

It was a lonely day today. I dropped Adia off at school and decided to tackle my small but important Target list. As I parked my jeep, I thought nothing of the red carts and hustle and bustle of this store. I've been here many times—before and after Piper. Nothing new. As I walked in and grabbed a cart, I saw the sale racks! They were clearing out their summer clothes, and since I don't fit anything but my pregnancy clothes, I thought it would be great to find some real clothes to fit into for the time being (until we tackle a diet). Walking in, and then out, of the dressing room...I felt defeated. Seriously? What size were those pants that actually FIT? I looked in the mirror in the dressing room at my body that was so misshaped, compared to last year at this time. I have journeyed through a pregnancy, through the cravings, and ended up here...standing in front of a mirror, flabby, post-prego, with no child. I miss her.

As I pushed my cart to find some teething tablets for Adia's two-year molars, my vision caught the sweet pink and brown car seat in the next isle. I've been tough, for the most part. I have put on my "tough skin" and walked up and down these aisles. Today, I felt vulnerable. I wanted my baby girl. I wanted to need a car seat. I wanted to be buying formula, to be pushing Piper around with me, and to have some proof as to why I'm still wearing maternity clothes. My heart was aching.

We got in the car around 7 that night and headed to New Braunfels for Labor Day weekend. As we hit tremendous amounts of traffic, Adia got frustrated in the back seat. "Out! Out!" I began to pray that the Lord would comfort her. As she continued to fidget and kick and scream, I began to get angry. I know that through all of this, anger has really not overwhelmed me (by the grace of God). But I realized that although I do not get angry about Piper, when God seems to not hear my seemingly "small" requests, I get angry! Frustration sets in. "Why can't you just fix this for me NOW? I'm not asking much, Lord!" I know how foolish that sounds and how petty these small things are in the grand scheme of His ultimate plan. But selfish emotions are part of our human nature—part of this broken and fallen world.

Arriving in New Braunfels, we played and Adia smiled. It was refreshing to, again, be surrounded by sweet family. What a precious gift! As she laughed and giggled, it hit the late hours of evening, and I got her ready for bed. As I lay with her as she nodded off, the recent visit here began to run through my head. Last time we were here, we were burying our baby girl. Last time we were here, we were filled with emotions that were so fresh and new. Flowers were ordered, the ground was dug open, and a little white casket was placed with a headstone that said, "Piper Kay Brawner." Tears began to pour down my face. My chest began to heave up and down. From Target to lying with Adia, today had been a day filled with a yearning for her baby sister to be in my arms too.

The darkness of the night surrounded me as I shut the door to the room of my sleeping baby girl and looked in the eyes of my precious husband. "I need to go. I need to go." As he looked at my tear-stained face, I'm not sure if he understood what I meant until I grabbed the keys and headed out the door. He grabbed his shoes and sat in the passenger seat next to me. The clock in the car said 1 a.m., and as we started that windy dark road toward the cemetery, the car was quiet. All I could hear were the thoughts spinning in my head and the deafening silence. Finally, from the quietness, my husband asked, "What are you thinking?"

I stuttered, as I began to share through shaking words, and he listened. I shared that my heart feels like this is our responsibility. This is our baby girl. We can't be here to make sure her grave is beautiful, and I feel like we need to go—now! We are her mother and father. She is our baby. We buried her. She is ours. And the fact that we cannot be the ones to ensure that her grave is the most beautiful one out there rips my heart to pieces. So, I need to go. I need to be there. I need to see her grave. The car became silent again.

The turns and windy roads were filled with heartache. Every

turn, we knew, brought us closer to the truth. As I turned my brights on, I wanted to hear from his heart. I was sitting there bawling, tears streaming down my face and soaking my shirt in complete attempt to be transparent with my precious, sweet husband. What on earth is he thinking? Finally, I muster up the courage to tell him if he doesn't want to share—that's fine and dandy. But that it is going to put a wedge in our relationship that we will never be able to pry loose. I, as his wife, need him to share with me how he feels…even though it is difficult for him! I need to hear! I need to be a part. I need him to open up and pour out. And as he eventually began to share, what I realized is that for him, to pour out his soul is like pouring salt on his wounds. It will heal it, but it hurts him so badly.

Pulling up to the cemetery in the pitch black, we saw our baby girls' pink bush glowing. We bought a solar bush with beautiful pink flowers that soaks up sun in the daylight so it can glow beautifully through the night. At 1:30 a.m. it was the brightest light out there. We walked up to where we buried her not too long ago. As we both stood there, alone in this dark cemetery, we fell to our knees and wept. His heart broke all over again. My soul ached so deeply. We flooded the dirt with our tears. Our bodies mourned, and I just kept rubbing the flowers on her bush, wishing it were her tiny little hands. I looked at my husband's body, crouched over his daughter's grave, and I was crushed. Here is my sweet, loving, precious, strong husband. He is the man I fell in love with so many years ago. Never did I think my heart would hurt so badly for this man I love him so deeply. He lost his daughter. He lost his baby girl. He can never walk her down the aisle or dance with her or hear her say, "Daddy." And as his body shook with grief over her grave that night, we wept tears of immense sorrow mixed with every other emotion imaginable.

I looked at him and said, "If I could just hold her for the rest of my life, even if she didn't take one breath, I would. I would hold her. I want to hold her. Her sweet, perfect body is right here…a few feet below the ground! And I want to hold her!" Choking on my own words, he shared his anger and frustration. He looked around and in between sobs he shared that if he could haul a mattress out here, he would sleep with her so that she would not be alone. Then he stood, looked to the sky, and as we held one another he said, "But I know, she is not alone. She's in the most perfect place—and I know that. I know she is not alone." I let out a cry that was so intense and heartfelt and began to sob, "No, she's not alone. We are. We are the ones alone out here. We are alone, left in this world without her. We're standing here alone, in this cemetery, without our baby—alone. But she…she is not." His tears poured onto my shoulders and mine onto the ground. We stood there, holding one another in the pitch black of night—alone.

September 5, 2011

We took bright and beautiful flowers out to the grave for Piper today. As we walked around the grocery store to pick them out, I thought I would be okay. But the fact of the matter is—we were deciding on flowers to put on our daughters grave. It sucked.

Tears began to fill my eyes as we came across the brightest flowers in the entire department. They were full of joy and looked like they could make anyone smile. They did. I smiled as I gently picked them up. We scanned the flower department, and Dave and my eyes met as we saw a Winnie the Pooh balloon. I could barely speak, but when Dave asked me if I wanted to get it for her, I just nodded my head yes.

When we checked out, the girl asked Dave, "Do you mind me asking, what does July 27, 2011 on your tattoo mean?" She was staring at the top of his wrist. As he smiled, he told her about

Piper. I'm sure she wished she hadn't asked…sooner or later we would get better at sharing the news. Or maybe not. It will always be a bomb that we drop in someone's lap.

In the heat of the morning, we drove the long road to her grave. As we bathed the ground in tears yet again, we filled it with the bright colors of joy and a balloon that her sister would have insisted upon giving her. Our hearts ache to be closer, as her parents, to take care of that little piece of land that will always hold her earthly body. We wish we could visit out there to make sure it remains beautiful. Maybe someday we will be closer.

As we tearfully got in the car, her balloon blowing in the wind, Dave's gentle heart looked at me and poured out. "It's so sad… all these graves for these babies, and there is nothing on them. I know it is a loss that you don't want to recognize, but we have to do it—to keep coming to see Piper. Look at these graves with nothing on them at all." His heart was so sad. So together, we counted 36 little graves holding bodies of babies that have gone to be with our Father. Thirty five plus our Piper Kay. We know it is just dirt. We know it is a grave, and there is death and not life. But Piper will share, through her death. And we will find 36 little "somethings" for her to share with her friends out there. You better believe it.

September 7, 2011

We had to go back home again. The long stretch from New Braunfels to our front door was made even longer by the stop-and-go traffic and a screaming two-year old. I'm lost. My words are so scattered in my head and in my heart. Someone asked me yesterday if I was angry. I told them I'm really not…until I see Adia hurting or hear her crying. I don't get angry until I see a woman who is smoking in the face of her newborn. I feel as if I've undertaken a huge surgery and my heart has been ripped from my chest. Instead of my heart, God has chosen to insert the heart of His Son. Now I see pain on the faces that most may miss. I feel sorrow and loss when I hear of others' life tragedies. My heart breaks when I see people living so hastily and not cherishing the life that has been granted them. And I get angry when people spit in the face of goodness and choose selfishness over what is best for their child, their spouse, and their family. A new heart. It is not my own, nor does it feel like my own. It is very—strange.

Two nights ago, Adia continued waking up every other hour. As I rocked her and finally lay with her in the spare bed, she tossed and turned. She could not breathe because she was so stuffed up. At times, I would lay my hand on her chest to make sure that it was moving up and down. I felt her little heartbeat, and my stomach hit the floor. That is what I never got to feel with Piper. That is what I yearned for and what is still so unreal. She lost her heartbeat. As Adia flipped over again and again, I picked her up and cradled her in my arms. I rocked her and began to cry tears of frustration and sadness, anger and sorrow. In my arms, her little body calmed down, and her breathing became closer to normal than what it had been all night thus far. My heart was breaking— again. I stumbled, by myself, into the living room, in complete darkness, and fell to my knees. "What more do you want from me, Lord?" I cried to him, with my broken voice. I sobbed and sobbed. "What more do you want from me? Please, God. Please do not take my child! I need Adia. I need her to sleep. I need to sleep. What more can I give?" I wept there, on my knees. My heart felt like it was shattered in a million different pieces.

My sweet husband heard me and came and sat with me through my aching tears. "I know, honey. I know." He held me, and then he lifted me up. We stood and watched our living breathing baby girl roll around on the bed, and we held each other in silence. She is entrusted to us. She is ours for only a short while on this earth. She is our precious gift. She is our Adia. Our hearts are broken right now. Although they have begun to heal, pieces of it are still a mess. And as we stood there that night over Adia and held one another, it was a reminder of how we stood there over Piper's grave a few nights before...together, in the darkness, holding each other. We will stand watch over our baby girls. Forever.

September 11, 2011

That date will always ring in my mind. September eleventh. I remember when the world changed this day—10 years ago. I was in College Station, on the Texas A&M campus. As we heard about what was going on, I remember sitting in amazement, watching the big screens they had placed around the MSC. There were so many college students crowded in the building, watching in horror and silence. And today, I sat in church thinking about how many families were impacted by loss on that day.

It seems like there is so much tragedy in this world. It is broken. It is hurting. It is falling. Thankfully, this world is not our own. As we were challenged to remember those on 9/11, we were also challenged to remember that our God is still at work. The pastor made a statement—we can choose to either remember only the grief or remember God's hand of help in the midst of the difficult times.

It is important to remember. Standing in the cemetery the other day, gazing over the graves of these children, it was hard not to notice that maybe some have tried to *not* remember their huge loss. I know that it hurts, deeply. I know that losing Piper straight up stinks. I wish she were here. But I do not ever want to forget her. I want to remember.

I can't help but wonder how many of those people that lost someone dear to him or her on 9/11 ten years ago were left alone, untouched by the hand of anyone. I wonder how many there were that had no one extend love, a shoulder squeeze, or a hug. I know that in the midst of our loss, there have been many who have chosen to step back from us. They have chosen to leave us alone and not call or text or email. They do not want to remember, because it hurts. We *have* to remember. It pierces and aches, but we have to remember. And as someone behind us in church sniffled and cried, I prayed for them. I couldn't catch them before they were out the door to squeeze their shoulder or shake their hand, but I prayed. And as the pastor shared about a girl in the community that had gone to bed and never woken up, our eyes immediately filled with falling tears, and I decided to send a card, even though I do not know them at all. Why? Because I've lost. I've loved and lost. And Piper Kay is important enough to remember...therefore, everyone's lost one is important enough to remember. It hurts, it yields tears, and it brings painful memories. But that is okay. I refuse to be one that runs instead of remembers. For those out there on this tragic day in our country that have loved and lost—I'm remembering right alongside you.

September 13, 2011

Just the name brings tears today. Piper. Why? Why so much pain on this earth? I know that we have sinned...and because of this, awful things entered the world. Oh, to take it all back. If we had only obeyed in the beginning, this heartache would be non-existent. Our Piper would be in our arms right now, and we would be rocking her and mixing bottles. Instead, there is a deafening silence that fills the walls of our house. Adia plays, and we try our hardest to do all that we can with her. But sometimes, when she plays by herself, we wait to hear the cry of her sister. It will never come.

When will this go away? When will our heart stop aching to hold and know our daughter? When will this become a reality? I can sit here and honestly say—I think this is our new reality.

We are so lonely. We are so tired of being strong. Our bodies ache, and our minds make no sense. We feel like we have to be "tough" in this situation and stand strong. We are not. We are barely hanging on to the God that created us. We look up and don't understand the plans he has for us, but in his face, we see that we can trust him in the midst of the darkness. We know that his hand holds us and that, although we may feel like we are falling, we're not. We can ask "Why?" all day long. "Why nine months? Why a girl? Why is she gone? Why do we have to hurt? Why can't Adia have a sister? Why did this happen to us when we've been following you faithfully? Why now? Why here? Why?" And the answers? Some we may never know. Some we may be granted glimpses of as Piper impacts the lives of those around us. But most of these answers require us to hold tight to the fact that he *is* the great "I AM" even though we will never understand it all.

September 15, 2011

I was in the hospital today, but for a very different reason than those of seven short weeks ago. I was there to celebrate with a friend the birth of her healthy, chunky, precious baby girl. As I woke up this morning, all I could do was smile in anticipation of seeing her and her baby girl. I sped to the hospital as quickly as possible and eagerly, nervously pushed the "up" arrow for the seventh floor. As I walked by the nursery on the way to her room, I stopped. Breath. Life. Babies. I peered through the window for a long time, watching the nurses holding and coddling the newborns. I smiled and was filled with love. I was so happy for those mothers, although I knew only one. I wondered what it would have been like to see Piper with the peachy pink skin and ruffled dark hair, swaddled behind that glass. And as I stood there, I wondered where they had placed my precious baby when she spent her short time that day in the nursery. Her skin was a much different color, her movements were non-existent, and her little body was lifeless. But I know they took extra special care of her in her earthly nursery.

As I spent time hopefully being an encouragement to my friend and not a giddy annoyance, I realized that this curse of labor that came when sin entered the world was well worth it. Although awful, painful, and hard to recover from, laboring for your child is a pure blessing when you are able to look into their face, kiss the top of their head and say, "I love you!"

My heart outpoured with love, hope, and joy today. Although I missed Piper terribly, I was given a glimpse into the joys of seeing Christ and knowing that Jesus loves the little children. *Oh, Father, rock her till we get there. Tell her we love her. Kiss her and hold her...and while you're at it, hold us too. We need it.*

September 21, 2011

I'm sitting here watching the minutes on the clock tick by. My time at home is running out, and I count down the days till I have to arrive ready for work. I woke up in the middle of the night and rolled over to see 3:30 a.m. in bright fluorescent numbers shining...haunting. Tick. Tick. Tick.

I do not understand what God is doing in me. I can imagine the lives he will impact through Dave and me. But what is he doing in me? I feel a mess as I await the daunting task of walking those halls

143

of school and announce, "Hello class, my name is..." Will I ever be ready? No. Will it ever be fair? No. Will I ever understand? I don't think so.

As I lay there with the tick tock of the clock rolling, I thought of how many giggles I'd be enjoying right now if Piper were laying here with me. I want to curl up in a ball, scream, break plates, and tell everyone to leave me alone and that my life stinks. But I know I cannot do that. For one, we have Adia. But we also know that, although this life is awful right now, God has a bigger plan. Why does it have to hurt? Why does it have to suck? Why does it have to include pain and suffering? Honestly, I don't know. But I do know...I must keep walking in the midst of this storm.

Some days I'm crawling in the dust. Some days I'm laying, flat in the middle of the road, not budging. Other days, I can walk at a somewhat healthy pace. But in every day I know, I've got to keep going. There may be no light at the end of the tunnel that I can see, but surely it's there...right Lord? Grant me a glimpse of your glory. I'm begging.

I wonder if I had Piper here snuggling next to me, cooing and cuddling, screaming and pooping...would I be living in the midst of a complaining spirit? Would I complain that she cried through the night, that she was growing too quickly out of her clothes, or that she eats/cries/poops too much? Right now, in her death, I feel I've got the *right* to complain. But that is so untrue. I am not called to live in that spirit, no matter my circumstances. Oh, that these complaints would bleed dry from me, so that even in the midst of the horror of death I face daily, I may overcome it—moment by moment—and without complaints. Then one day, when I look into the face of my beautiful Piper, I can say, "I have joyfully waited to see you, baby girl!" God has given me blessings, although seemingly few right now—and not at all in the form that I desire. But they are blessings, and I must learn to turn them into praise.

Help me to see the blessings, Lord. Grant me a glimpse of your glory. Help me to walk with steps of praise rather than grumblings. I don't understand you or your vast plan for life here on earth. But help me to walk it successfully, even though every step hurts.

"For God is working in you, giving you the desire and the power to do what pleases him. Do everything without complaining and arguing, so that no one can criticize you. Live clean, innocent lives as children of God, shining like bright lights in a world full of crooked and perverse people," Philippians 2:13-15.

October 23, 2011

"Holy, Holy, Holy is the Lord God Almighty." As we stood singing this song in church today, tears fell like rain. The same words Piper sings every moment of every day, I shared with her in praise to our Savior. I felt like God allowed her to lean down and whisper to me, "Mommy—I love you. I'm okay. Just do your job on earth like Jesus has asked you to do and come see me. I'm waiting for you!" Grace like rain fell at that moment. The anger I've felt, the pain and hurt that pierces so deeply, turned to pride and joy in that moment. Through my tiny breath I whispered, "Piper, can you tell your daddy you're okay, too?"

It does not get easier without her. The pain may subside. We may learn to cope and deal in our own way. But the emptiness without her laughter, her smile, and touching her skin to our face will be something missed forever.

Standing in church and praising our God brings instant tears. It has taken time, but the Lord has provided His gracious hand to hold us upright and continue walking this path before us. I love the Lord. There is no part of me that thinks He has done this to me. I know He is a good and gracious God and would never desire anyone to endure the same pain He had to face as He watched Christ die before His eyes. But this is a fallen, broken, messed up world. Satan prowls around seeking to steal, kill, and destroy. "Holy, Holy, Holy is the Lord God Almighty, who was and is and is to come." All I know is that on the day I am called home, I will be ready. And as I walk this earth, waiting to be called home, I will do what Jesus has asked me to do. Some days, it may simply be surviving those 24 hours. Other days, it may be ministering to a room of people. I know that when He calls, I will answer.

"Then I heard the voice of the Lord saying, 'Whom shall I send? And who will go for us?' And I said, 'Here am I. Send me!' " Isaiah 6:8.

November 10, 2011

We just found out our baby girl has to have surgery! What? Really? What more can we handle right now? I guess the Lord thinks that we can handle this and so…we will step into in faith, knowing it is the best for our little angel.

The ENT doctor we took her to in Dallas suggested that our precious Adia undergo surgery on November 16. We are hurting that she has to do it, but grateful that the doctor will do it so quickly. She is getting her adenoids and tonsils out, as well as having her turbinates shaved down (extra tissue in her nose taken out). This is all due to "sleep apnea" and her inability to breathe at night!

She is a mouth breather, she snores, and her allergies are crazy (just like her daddy!). The doc said since we had tried everything he would have suggested already, and her poor little nose is still closed tight without the ability to breath. I feel like an awful parent! All this time, those restless nights of tossing and turning, have been due to her little bodies inability to breathe in and out.

My soul is reacting very different to this news. We are begging God not to take her from us and to bless the surgery and her healing process. It is tender to our hearts. We know God is God, and we know it is best for Adia...we just hate that she has to go through it. I will remain in constant petition before our Almighty God to keep my child with us in this world, for I cannot bear to lose another.

November 16, 2011

Well, surgery went well. Recovery was, by far, horrible. Because of the turbinate reduction portion of it, she bled and bled and bled. Coming off the anesthesia, she was awful, horrible, and so sad—the most awful thing I've seen with her. We were covered in her blood. She was so sad, so scared, so confused. It took a long time in recovery for them to allow us to go in and see her. The doctor asked us if she'd had numerous throat infections because the tonsils that were removed were so beat up. Our answer? No. How did we miss that? All this time, we thought it was teething or molars or...all this time, it had been her throat? Oh sweet Adia Michele. You are one tough cookie!

As I held her in my arms and rocked her in the recliner, covered in her blood, my heart ached in agony, wishing I could take all the pain from her. I think that is the heartbeat of any parent. We wish we could take it all away from them. How much more does our Heavenly Father love us and desire to keep us from the pain?

I am certain that this will help. In the stench of blood and the midst of pure pain, I am most positive that our precious Adia will recover quickly and finally—rest.

Thank you, dear Jesus, for not taking Adia from us. Thank you for allowing her to remain here with us. We promise to treasure her and love her, always pointing her to the hope of you.

November 27, 2011

Four months to the day. By now, many have forgotten that we've lost a daughter. Most have moved on with their lives. We are still here, attempting to make it through day by day. I think we all thought that time would heal. Really, time has made the wound deeper. Reality without our Piper has sunk in so deep that it penetrates to parts of our souls we did not know could ache with pain. We mourn and grieve so intensely. Day by day, we wake up and continue to put one foot in front of the other and make it through in a, hopefully, God-honoring way. Our hearts resonate with the growls of anger...and yet it is an anger that we have not known before. It is His righteous anger. There is no way you can endure a loss and not grieve without experiencing anger. Am I angry with my husband? No. Am I angry with God? Ultimately... no. Although Satan may attempt his best to make us think that, it is not true. I have realized that it is His holy anger. This world is fallen, one in which death should never have entered in the first place. How can He not mourn as we mourn? How can he not cry as we weep, barely able to stand? How can His heart not break when He sees His children enduring part of sin that He never intended in the beginning? It's not Him. It is not our God that has taken her or left us. He is there. Although we may not feel it all the time, He is holding us. He promises to never ever leave us or forsake us. And He knows the pain of losing a child. He knows the pain that we go through every day, the heartbreak of life without her, and the sadness that has nestled deep within us. He is oh-so-familiar with this pain. Are we angry with that God? No. No we are not. We are angry that sin has brought death.

Why has this happened? Why to us? Why can't we hold her right now? We will never understand. He tells us to trust Him with all our hearts and not to lean on our own understanding in Proverbs 3. We must believe that because it is truth. We have to trust that His plans are greater. I know that through this, He has granted us a part of His heart that bleeds with compassion beyond anything we could have imagined. Pain, heartache, sorrow, or even a day of sadness strikes my heart to a new level now.

This journey through loss has just begun. I see loss through different eyes now. Everyone, at some point or another, will have to face it in his or her own lives. Each story is different. Each loss is unique. Each pain is relevant. And with eyes of compassion and a heart that hurts ever so quickly, I now understand that this is a lifelong journey that our family will walk through. This is the beginning of a life without Piper Kay Brawner. This is a family stricken with grief and a pain that will never be taken away. There is a void that will never be filled and a sadness that, although it may subside, will never disappear. And that is okay. The tears will always come. There will be good days and bad days. What we know is that, although our emotions will be a roller-coaster ride, our God is not. He is faithful. He is truth. And even though it hurts to trust sometimes, we must. He is the only true Rock; He is the only true foundation; and though the storms come and go, He stays. His hand is there to hold us tight, and even if we are pushing Him away or trying to run, deep in our soul we know—He is there, and we are held...forevermore.

"Have mercy on me, LORD, for I am faint; heal me, LORD, for my bones are in agony. My soul is in deep anguish. How long, LORD, how

long? I am worn out from all my groaning. All night long I flood my bed with weeping and drench my couch with tears. My eyes grow weak with sorrow...The LORD has heard my weeping. The LORD has heard my cry for mercy. The LORD accepts my prayer." Psalm 6:2-3, 6-7a, 9.

December 31, 2011

It's time to bring the New Year in. 2012. Can't believe it. As fireworks go off, illegally, next door, and we crawl under the blankets at, oh, 9:30 p.m., I reflect on the blessings of what makes *Team Piper* a team. I have people who have rallied with Dave and me in constant prayer and support. I send email updates, long or short, and share life with them. Hopefully they want to hear. They have been my *Team Piper*—the rock, the ones that hold my hands up when I feel like they are going to fall. They are the backbone of prayer that moves one foot in front of the other. They are my team.

Christmas without our daughter's smiles, laughs, giggles, and red Christmas dresses was not fun. It was great to be with family and friends, but missing Piper was constantly on our hearts.

A few days before Christmas, her headstone for her grave came in. It is beautiful. Dave and I went out there Christmas Eve to decorate her sweet tree with ribbons and bows, snowflakes and ornaments...all things that we should have been able to do with her. We wanted her tree to be beautiful, just like she is. We wanted it to shout, "Joy"...just as she is. And it does. As we walked out there to her grave on the dreary eve, tears joined the raindrops that fell from Heaven. We drenched her little grave with conversation, beauty, and tears. It is beautiful, peaceful place in Texas' hill country.

And then...we received a call that her well in Uganda was

completed. Tears of joy, sorrow, and parental pride sung in our soul. What an amazing, amazing joy to know that through our loss, Piper Kay Brawner will be a part of providing clean well water for people in Uganda. What a perfect Christmas gift for them this year.

I dreaded the thought of attending the Christmas Eve service without Piper. We normally attend Oakwood Baptist Church in New Braunfels. Over the past few years, they have incorporated into their services a time to remember those who are not with us during the Christmas season. I knew the moment would come, an invitation to light a candle in memory of your loved one. As the time came, Dave and I picked up Adia and limped to the front. With no breath in my chest and with my hands shaking uncontrollably, we spilled tears as Adia lit one candle—Piper's candle. As the three of us, faces alit with the glow of that candle, stood at the front of the church, time stood still for a moment. Shaking and barely able to walk, we somehow made it to the back of the room in a corner. We held tightly to Adia and sobbed. Our family of four, with only three remaining, mourned that Christmas Eve. It was a thick reminder that this is only the beginning of a lifetime of moments without our sweet Piper.

A new year—without the one we love so dearly. It hurts to think about it. I'm cringing at the thought of tackling 365 more days. And yet, that peace that hovers so gently around our household is calming me now. Every year will be another 365 days to tackle. It will be a choice we will *always* have to make—will we live it in anger, hurt and bitterness? Or will we choose to walk in the newness of Christ? I may limp through life. I may be paralyzed in some moments. I may be able to run in other moments. But I know that I will be healed, and someday soon, I will be called home to spend eternity with the ones I love so dearly.

Jeremiah 29:10-14 (NLT)

This is what the LORD says: "You will be in Babylon for seventy years. But then I will come and do for you all the good things I have promised, and I will bring you home again. For I know the plans I have for you," says the LORD. "They are plans for good and not for disaster, to give you a future and a hope. In those days when you pray, I will listen. If you look for me wholeheartedly, you will find me. I will be found by you," says the LORD. "I will end your captivity and restore your fortunes. I will gather you out of the nations where I sent you and will bring you home again to your own land.

From Isaiah 61 (NLT)

The Spirit of the Sovereign LORD is upon me,
for the LORD has anointed me
to bring good news to the poor.
He has sent me to comfort the brokenhearted
and to proclaim that captives will be released
and prisoners will be freed.
He has sent me to tell those who mourn
that the time of the LORD's favor has come,
and with it, the day of God's anger against their enemies.
To all who mourn in Israel,
he will give a crown of beauty for ashes,
a joyous blessing instead of mourning,
festive praise instead of despair.
In their righteousness, they will be like great oaks
that the LORD has planted for his own glory.

From Psalm 139 (NIV)

You have searched me, LORD, and you know me.
You know when I sit and when I rise;
you perceive my thoughts from afar.
You discern my going out and my lying down;
you are familiar with all my ways.
Before a word is on my tongue
you, LORD, know it completely.
You hem me in behind and before,
and you lay your hand upon me.
Such knowledge is too wonderful for me,
too lofty for me to attain.

For you created my inmost being;
you knit me together in my mother's womb.
I praise you because I am fearfully and wonderfully made;
your works are wonderful, I know that full well.
My frame was not hidden from you
when I was made in the secret place,
when I was woven together in the depths of the earth.
Your eyes saw my unformed body;
all the days ordained for me were written in your book
before one of them came to be.
How precious to me are your thoughts, God!
How vast is the sum of them!
Were I to count them, they would outnumber the grains of sand—
when I awake, I am still with you.

Resources

that have ministered to our souls

Now I Lay Me Down to Sleep Ministries, www.nilmdts.org or www.nowilaymedowntosleep.org

Grief Share 365 Daily Emails, www.griefshare.org

Holden Uganda, www.holdenuganda.com

Hope Mommies, www.hopemommies.org

Deer Creek Camp, www.deercreekcamp.com

Let God be God, Life-changing truths from the book of Job by Ray C. Stedman

"Held" recorded by Natalie Grant (written by Christa Wells); *Awaken* Album

"A Thousand Things" by Christa Wells, www.christawellsmusic. com

"The Luckiest" by Ben Folds; *Rockin' the Suburbs*

CPSIA information can be obtained at www.ICGtesting.com
Printed in the USA
LVOW060832080512

280719LV00001B/19/P